How to Win

in life, business, and everything else.

D1637613

Leading Edge Leadership Limited 2014

First published in 2014

by

Leading Edge Publications, London.

FOREWORD

A young boy enters a barber shop and the barber whispers to his customer "This is the dumbest kid in the world. Watch while I prove it to you."

The barber puts a £5 note in one hand and a £1 coin in the other, then calls the boy over and asks "Which do you want, son?"

The boy takes the £1 coin and leaves.

"What did I tell you?" said the barber. "That kid never learns!"

Later, when the customer leaves, he sees the same young boy coming out of the ice cream shop.

"Hey, son! May I ask you a question? Why did you take the £1 instead of the fiver?"

The boy licked his cone and replied, "Because the day I take the fiver, the game is over!"

Life is a game. So is business, and everything else.

Why do some people, and some businesses, always seem to come out on top while the rest look on and ask why? Is it confidence, intelligence, qualifications, hard work, perseverance, luck, or even good looks? All of these help, but winning goes much deeper than that, deep into the chemistry of who we are and how we act.

Muhammad Ali, one of the greatest boxers of our time, believes "Champions aren't made in the gyms. Champions are made from something they have deep inside them – a desire, a dream, a vision."

So what separates the winners from the losers in life, business and everything else?

We were all born to win but to be a winner you need to plan to win, prepare to win, and expect to win. Winning is a mindset. If you don't see yourself as a winner, then you cannot perform as a winner. This mindset was captured brilliantly by the response of ex-Manchester United manager Alex Ferguson when asked for his views by a television reporter after a very late goal saw Manchester United lose 2-1 at Chelsea:

We didn't lose; we just ran out of time.

To be a winner you have to learn the rules of the game and then you have to play better than anyone else.

Enjoy the read.

ACKNOWLEDGEMENTS

Thanks to all those winners in life, business, and everything else who believed this book was possible – you know who you are.

CONTENTS

Download Your FREE Bonus Chapter NOW!

Barack Obama's

3 Winning Secrets

Simply put the word **BARACK** in your subject title and send your email to:

info@leadingedgeleadership.com

How to Win — in life, business, and
everything else | JJ Lynch

Introduction

There is an innate desire within each of us to achieve in life. Some of us tap into this desire of achievement. Unfortunately for many others this desire remains dormant. Such people tend to let life act on them rather than act on life. A study by Bodenhamer and Hall[1] (1999) suggested that only 5% of the population of the USA had a clear idea about what they wanted to achieve in life. The authors made a powerful point by asking, "what do the other 95% do?" The answer is "work for the 5%." If you are one of the 5% you probably don't need to read this book. I guess your perusal of this book may suggest you're one of the greater mass wanting to be one of the 5%, so read on.

The first principle for winning in life, business and everything else is to take responsibility for the quality of your life. Winners recognise that responsibility. They never blame circumstances or conditions. Each one of us has control over three things in our life – the thoughts we think, the pictures we visualise and the actions we take (our behaviour). How we use these three things determines everything we experience.

Each of us was born with a life purpose. Many people wander through life accomplishing very little. Knowing your life purpose means you are doing what you are good at and accomplishing what is important to you. Most people don't get what they want because they haven't decided what they want. So, Principle 2 – define your purpose in life, what's important to you and what you want to accomplish.

In order to reach your accomplishments you need to have goals. Goal setting is incredibly important and crucial to being a winner. Achieving your goals is a realisation of your potential. However, the real value of reaching a goal lies not in the result achieved but in the journey you've walked and what it has made of you as a person. Principle 3 – have goals.

These first three principles are the core principles for winning in life, business, and everything else – taking responsibility for your life, defining your life purpose, and having goals. The four remaining principles are what we call the mindset principles – affirm yourself and others often, know what you excel at, surround yourself with winning people and always want to improve.

The prime need of every human being (and most organisations) is to be loved, valued and respected. All teaching begins with yourself. Do you love yourself? Do you value yourself? Do you respect yourself? When you answer yes to each of these questions you can truly affirm yourself, and, in turn, find it easy to affirm others. The fourth principle for a winning mindset is to affirm yourself, and others, often.

Show me a successful person and often you will find a person who is doing what they excel at. And doing it well. One of the key secrets to being a winner is to know what you have a flair for and do it. Principle 5 – know what you excel at, and do it.

Take a moment and think about the people you spend time with – at work, at home, or in your hobbies or social life. Are they enthusiastic, energetic, passionate, happy people? Are they interesting to talk to? Are they open to change, to learn? Do they put a smile on your face? We become like the people we spend most time with. If you want to be a winner you have to start hanging out with winning people. Free yourself from the negative influence of others. Surround yourself with people who will help you grow. Such people will bring out the best in you. Principle 6 – surround yourself with winning people.

The final principle for winning is to have the mindset of always wanting to improve. Being a winner means believing that things can always be better. Most people would prefer to cling to security than aim for the stars. Fear of failure, of ridicule, of embarrassment. However, there can be no success without failure. If you want to be a winner, you can't stand still. To do so means to be left behind. Time then to be your best – take responsibility, challenge the way things are, refuse to accept mediocrity, be innovative, passionate, strive for the winning line. Time to start – today!

PRINCIPLE 1

TAKE RESPONSIBILITY FOR YOUR LIFE

Winning is not a sometime thing; it is an all the time thing.

You don't win once in a while, you don't do things right once in a while, you do them right all of the time.

Winning is habit. Unfortunately, so is losing.

Vince Lombardi

YOUR LIFE: YOUR RESPONSIBILITY

There is only one person responsible for the quality of life you live. That person is you.

Look at the word responsibility – "response-ability" – the ability to choose your response. Winners recognise that responsibility. In his book *The 7 Habits of Highly Effective People*,[2] Stephen Covey tells us that, "We are responsible for our own lives." Every outcome you experience in life is the result of how you responded to an earlier event or events in your life - 10% of life is made up of what happens to you; 90% of life is decided by how you react to the 10%.

Winners do not blame circumstances or conditions. The playwright George Bernard Shaw said, "People are always blaming circumstances for what they are. I do not believe in circumstances. The people who get on in this world are the people who get up and look for the circumstances they want, and if they can't find them, make them." Choosing our response to circumstances will powerfully affect our circumstances. What characterises winners is that they don't let circumstances influence them; they influence the circumstances.

Life is a game. You can win in the game of life and you can lose. What separates the winners and losers in life is how they handle disappointment. Winning is not just about being ambitious – that's the easy part. Winning is about overcoming adversity and failure. The media magnet Sumner Redstone believes "Success is not built on success. It's built on failure. It's built on frustration. Sometimes it's built on catastrophe." Achievement in any field is impossible without setback. What separates the field is not the setback but how you respond to the setback. This is a point Stephen Covey emphasised time and again in his writings – it is not what happens to us but our response to what happens to us that counts. It is as true in life as it is in business and everything else.

Each one of us has control over three things in our life – the thoughts we think, the pictures we visualise and the actions we take (our behaviour). How you use these three things determines everything you experience. You will never be a winner as long as you continue to blame someone or something else for your lack of success. If you want to be a winner, you have to be truthful with yourself – it is you who took the actions, thought the thoughts, created the feelings and made the choices that got you to where you are now. It was you!

When you reach the point of fully accepting and saying "I am what I am today because of the choices I made yesterday" only then are you truly taking 100% responsibility.

Life is a game. You can win in the game of life and you can lose.

It is the ability to choose which makes us human.

Madeline L'Engle

THE ABILITY TO CHOOSE

Man's Search for Meaning[3] by Viktor Frankl is a small book but so very powerful. Frankl, an Austrian psychotherapist, survived the Nazi concentration camps while so many around him perished. But he never lost hope. His book reflects on what it was that helped him survive — his ability to choose how he responded to the horrendous circumstances he found himself in. They could strip him of everything but his greatest human freedom — the ability to choose. Frankl writes "Everything can be taken from a man but one thing, the last of the human freedoms to choose one's attitude in any given set of circumstances, to choose one's own way."

The most important of all our traits is the power we have to choose. To choose how we live. To choose what we say. To choose what we eat. To choose how we will view and consider a circumstance. While we are free to choose our actions, we are not free to choose the consequences of those actions. Some of our choices may bring consequences we would rather have lived without. If we had the choice to make over again, we would make it differently. We call these choices mistakes.

Mistakes are opportunities for learning. Benjamin Franklin, one of the founding fathers of the United States, said that we should not fear mistakes because it is through mistakes that we get to know failure. Oscar Wilde expressed such thinking beautifully when he said, "Experience is simply the name we give our mistakes." It is only through experiencing failure that we get to experience the real joy of winning. Hilary Clinton, former United States Secretary of State, echoed this sentiment when she said, "Going out and playing football or baseball with the boys, when I was a tomboy, was a great way to learn about winning and losing, and most girls didn't have that experience."

Each day we have the opportunity to make a great many choices. And the way we make those choices shapes who we become.

Mistakes are opportunities for learning.

When we do the best that we can, we never know what miracle is wrought in our life, or in the life of another.

Helen Keller

BE THE BEST YOU CAN BE

Jack was my A-Level English teacher. He is the teacher I remember most fondly.

Jack was an enthusiast. He taught by example, the most powerful form of teaching. And when every lesson finished and we tidied up our books he always reminded us as we went out the door – "Boys, be the best you can be." That phrase has stuck with me for life.

A manager once asked his mentor "What do I have to do to be the best I can be?" The mentor replied: "It is not the ***doing,*** it is the ***being*** that counts." So how does one **be** the best you can be? Being the best you can be is not a thing. You cannot buy it, fill a bucket with it or give it away. Being the best you can be is an attitude, a belief, a philosophy, and a mindset. So is winning. Winning starts with you and ends with you, because everyone has the ability within them to be the best they can be – and to be a winner.

How do you feel when you've given of your best? How do you feel when you've put in a good day's work at home or in the office? How do you feel when you've made someone feel good? It feels great. It always does. It reminds me of the words of Martin Luther King Jnr. who said: "If a man is called to be a street sweeper, he should sweep streets even as Michelangelo painted, or as Beethoven composed music or Shakespeare wrote poetry. He should sweep streets so well that all the hosts of heaven and earth will say, 'Here lived a great sweeper who did his job well'."

My grandmother had a beautiful phrase that she repeated often, "There will never be anyone else quite like you." Others might try to copy the way you think, the way you dress or the way you act. But no matter how hard they try, they will never be you. There is no one else quite like you. And because there will never be anyone else quite like you, there will never be a better time to be the best you than now. Go out today, and everyday, and be the best you can be. Have a winning mindset. You won't regret it.

There will never be anyone else quite like you.

Our deepest fear is not that we are inadequate.

Our deepest fear is that we are powerful beyond measure.

Marianne Williamson

YOU HAVE UNLIMITED CAPACITY

There are no limits to what you can achieve. The only person who sets limits for you is you. All the words we associate with limits are negative words – keep out, stop, never. When you limit yourself you destroy your potential and seek safety. As Eleanor Roosevelt said "No one can make you feel inferior without your consent". Seek out your best and discover the wonderful abilities that lie within you.

Henry Ford said, "Whether you think you can or you think you can't, you're right." Great quote. Think positively – I can, I will, I want to. There are many wonderful examples of people stretching themselves to their absolute physical and mental ability. Think of the great Olympian Michael Phelps who won eight gold medals in Beijing in 2008 to add to the six gold medals he won in Athens in 2004. Before 1954 it was believed no runner could ever break the four-minute mile barrier. But after Roger Bannister broke it many more proved it could be done. Why? Because Bannister showed people what could be done.

Our beliefs drive our actions. Our thinking creates our world. Think small and you'll act small. Think big and you'll act big. In 1980 Bill Gates said Microsoft would put a computer in every home and on every desk. And they did. Richard Branson says he will fly people to the moon for their holidays with his company Virgin Galactic. Branson dares to dream. So did Bill Gates. Winners see no limits.

Michelangelo said, "The greatest danger for most of us is not that our aim is too high and we miss it, but that it is too low and we reach it."

Aim high, because winners always do.

Our beliefs drive our actions.

There are no shortcuts to any place worth going.

Beverly Sills

THERE ARE NO SHORTCUTS TO WINNING

Reality shows have dominated our television screens over the last decade. They started with Big Brother and Pop Idol to be followed by The X-Factor and Strictly Come Dancing among many other dubious and eccentric versions. Shortcuts to glory and fame, a fast track path to winning. Glory, fame and success don't come that easily and as the reality shows have shown, albeit with a few exceptions, most winners disappear as quickly as they arrive.

We live in a world where easy is fashionable. We want to be spectacularly fit but we don't want to have to exercise regularly to get there. We want to be successful in our careers but we look for ways to get there without having to work hard and be disciplined. Nothing comes for free because there is no such thing as "free time".

You need to practise to be a winner. Practice demands discipline. The finest things in life take patience, focus, effort and sacrifice. There are no shortcuts. Behind every extraordinary achievement you will always discover extraordinary desire and discipline. Winning in life, business and everything else requires sacrifices. Most people give up too early. A true sign of maturity is the ability to give up instant gratification for a much more spectacular pleasure down the road. David Beckham scored a wonderful free-kick goal in the dying minutes for England against Greece that sent England to the 2002 World Cup finals just as they were staring shock elimination in the face. The beauty of the execution of Beckham's free kick was a sight to savour – what we didn't see were the countless hours of practising free kicks on the training field that Beckham religiously adhered to.

Every journey of a thousand miles begins with one small step. We are at our best when we are most challenged. In 1962 Kennedy threw down the gauntlet by challenging America to put a man on the moon by the end of the decade. "One small step for man, one giant leap for mankind" were the famous words spoken by Neil Armstrong at 0256 GMT on 21 July 1969 as he walked onto the surface of the moon – only in time have we truly realised the magnitude of the effort that went on behind the scenes for the previous seven years to make this happen.

The best among us – the winners in life – make it all look so easy and effortless. But like the graceful swan as it glides along the water what you don't get to see is all the planning, hard work, coordination and near flawless execution taking place below the surface. Yes, there are no shortcuts to winning.

Behind every extraordinary achievement you will always find extraordinary desire and discipline.

The most difficult instrument to play in the orchestra is second fiddle.

Leonard Bernstein

NEVER REST ON YOUR LAURELS

Nothing fails like success. You are most vulnerable when you are winning. Winning can breed complacency, casualness, contempt, and most of all – arrogance. When people and businesses win they forget about the things that got them to the winner's podium in the first place. They stop being creative and innovative, stop working hard, and stop taking risks. They go on the defensive spending their time protecting their success rather than staying true to the very things that made them winners in the first place.

Marks & Spencer are a great example of a high street brand that rested on their laurels. While they dithered and lived off their reputation, new brands, particularly in women's fashion, emerged to meet current trends. It was a wake-up call to M&S and ever since they have been seeking to wow back customers. They are finding the challenge difficult because when you rest on your laurels you soon become a follower rather than a leader. M&S are just one example – think BlackBerry and Kodak – while other high street brands like Woolworths have paid the ultimate price.

The more successful you and your organisation become, the more humble and customer-focused you need to become. You have to be always improving, always challenging norms, always attentive to what's happening around you. The moment you stop doing the very things that made you a winner is the very moment you begin to slide back into mediocrity again.

When you rest on your laurels you soon become a follower rather than a leader.

Example is not the main thing in influencing others.

It is the only thing.

Dr Albert Schweitzer

LEAD BY EXAMPLE

Lead by example. I know it's a cliché but one worth keeping in mind if you aspire to be a winner in life, business, and everything else. People don't follow titles; they follow leaders. The greatest sermon in life is not the one you hear but the one you see. It's easy to talk a good game. It's harder to live it. Ask Barack Obama!

Winners lead by example. Consistently. Persistently. Passionately. Winners talk less and do more. And in leading by example they don't worry who gets the credit for a job well done. They just get on and do the next thing that needs doing.

In the theatre it is said, "No role is a small role." And in life, as in business and everything else, no person is an insignificant person. The person who sweeps the floors or the person who makes the tea is every bit (if not more) significant than the most senior people in the organisation. I remember visiting a school and on a prominent noticeboard in the foyer was a beautiful sign that read, "In every good school, everybody matters."

What a beautiful sentiment.

In the best organisations, everyone does matter, and where such a culture exists, leading by example is the norm.

People don't follow titles, they follow leaders.

The most basic of all human needs is the need to understand and be understood.

The best way to understand people is to listen to them.

Ralph Nichols

BE A LISTENER

Great conversationalists are great listeners. Reflect for a moment on the letters of the word "listen". The letters also spell the word "silent". If you are not silent, you can't be listening.

Winners listen. And they listen remarkably well.

Listening is the one skill most people find difficult to master. Many of us listen to hear – to hear is to take notice of; to listen is to seek to understand.

Listening shows respect. Listening makes people feel special. Try it. Make a conscious decision to truly listen the next time you are in conversation with someone. Don't interrupt. Make eye contact. Don't rehearse your answer while they are speaking.

Many people are so self-focused that they fail to ask good questions when they meet another person. When you listen and ask questions you show humility. You show you are interested. It demonstrates that you are engaged. Most people's idea of listening is waiting until the other person has finished speaking so that they can interject.

Work at becoming not only a good listener, but also an excellent listener. You'll know yourself when you have listened well to someone. And you'll feel good about yourself because you will have so much more to offer. And you'll be liked and valued a lot more for it.

Great conversationalists are great listeners.

You give but little when you give of your possessions.

It is when you give of yourself that you truly give.

Kahil Gibran

BE A GIVER

Be a giver. Winners are givers. Think Bill Gates. By giving, you are living out a universal law – "life gives to the giver, and takes from the taker." The more you give, the more you get. If you want more love, more respect, more support and more compassion, give more love, give more respect, give more support and give more compassion. Be a mentor to others. Give back to your community. As a winner, the only way to get what you want is by helping enough people get what they want first. As Winston Churchill once said "We make a living by what we get, but we make a life by what we give."

Those who craft extraordinary careers are those who spend most of their time giving their best and going the extra mile. When you give you feel good about yourself. Albert Schweitzer said, "Life becomes harder for us when we live for others, but it also becomes richer and happier." But don't let others take advantage of your willingness to give. Don't carry other people's monkeys on your back. Learn to say no. Every time you say yes to something that is unimportant, you are saying no to something that is important. Be strong in yourself – don't seek the need to find affirmation through the approval of others. As Queen Victoria said "The important thing is not what they think of me, but what I think of them."

None of the world's greatest leaders were self-serving leaders – Gandhi, Mandela, Mother Teresa – all of them put the greater good of others first. Give to get. It's a very simple little statement but it's a statement that makes a big impact.

Those who craft extraordinary careers are those who spend most of their time giving their best and going the extra mile.

In three words I can sum up everything I've learned about life.

It goes on.

Robert Frost

THE MOST IMPORTANT WORDS

Words shape the way you feel. They influence the way you act. And they can either elevate you to your winning best or relegate you into a losing rut. No matter what life sends us, we are responsible for the way we respond. Starting with our words. Choose them well. Winners do. Always.

The six most important words:

"I admit that I was wrong."

The five most important words:

"You did a great job."

The four most important words:

"What do you think?"

The three most important words:

"May I help?"

The two most important words:

"Thank you."

The one most important word:

"We."

Words shape the way you feel.

We ourselves feel that what we are doing is just a drop in the ocean.

But the ocean would be less because of that missing drop.

Mother Teresa

THE MOST IMPORTANT ACTIONS

Actions shape what you achieve. They determine how successful you are, or why you fail. The actions that you take are influenced greatly by the beliefs that you hold. Our thinking dictates our beliefs and our beliefs determine how we respond (act). Here are some negative thoughts to be mindful of:

hopefully is an act of FEAR

might is an act of BEREAVEMENT

won't is an act of RETREAT

can't is an act of DEFEAT

Here is the mindset of a winner:

I want to is an act of DESIRE

I need to is an act of ACCOMPLISHMENT

I can is an act of POWER

I did is an act of ACHIEVEMENT

Winners excel and learn, not because they are told to, but because they want to.

Actions shape what you achieve.

PRINCIPLE 2

DEFINE YOUR PURPOSE IN LIFE

"Would you tell me please which way I ought to go from here?"

"That depends a good deal on where you want to get to," said the Cat.

"I don't much care where," said Alice.

"Then it does not matter which way you go," said the Cat.

from Alice in Wonderland by Lewis Carroll[4]

WHAT'S YOUR PURPOSE IN LIFE?

The purpose of life is a life of purpose.

Each of us is born with a life purpose. Winners understand what their life purpose is, and then pursue it with passion and enthusiasm.

Many people wander through life accomplishing very little. Knowing your life purpose means you are doing what you're good at and accomplishing what's important to you. Simon Cowell's life purpose is to make money in the music industry; Roger Federer's life purpose is to play beautiful tennis, win loads of Grand Slams and make money; Anita Roddick's life purpose was to provide cruelty-free cosmetics and run a profitable global business. My life purpose is to get people excited about leadership – and live very comfortably. I love what I do. I feel privileged to get paid for doing something I am passionate about. The greatest secret to winning is to figure out what you love to do and then organise your life around figuring out how to make a good living at it.

Most people don't get what they want because they haven't decided what they want. As a baby you knew exactly what you wanted. You knew when you were hungry so you cried until you got what you wanted. As you grew older you crawled around and moved towards whatever caught your eye. You knew what you wanted and went for it, without fear. When you were learning to walk, you fell. You got up and tried again. And again. So what happened? Somewhere along the way you were conditioned with the thoughts "don't do that", "don't go there" and "stop". And it is this conditioning that often colours how we feel, think and act.

What often stops people expressing their true desire is that they don't think they can make a living doing what they love to do. I have a good friend who worked in a large textile manufacturing company for years. He hated his work – same journey, same people, same conversations. He loved sports and every weekend his escape from his mundane week was to watch football or rugby or cricket. Eight years ago he decided he wanted something better. He wanted to enjoy work. He made up his mind to attend photography night classes. Today he is a full time sports photographer, making a good living – and happy.

The greatest secret to success is to figure out what you love to do and then organise your life around figuring out how to make a living at it.

*If you were born where I was born you would believe what I believe and if
I were born where you were born I would believe what you believe.*

Anonymous

WHAT ARE YOUR BELIEFS?

Beliefs are the essence of a person's behaviour. Beliefs are your operating principles for how you act. The actions you take, whether in your professional life, family life or personal life, are influenced greatly by the beliefs that you hold.

Your beliefs guide you in perceiving and interpreting your reality. Beliefs may be strongly held and they may enable you to act, or not. Beliefs are not cast in stone. They are only something you have put together in your mind. When they are not helpful to you, you can alter or completely change your beliefs. You once believed in Father Christmas! Your beliefs can be enabling beliefs that help you win in life or they can hold you back from the success that you can achieve.

Giraffes are the world's tallest animals. They also have the longest legs of any animal in the world. Giraffes give birth standing up and when a baby giraffe emerges into the world it is immediately faced with a six-foot drop, and is almost certainly dropped on its head. At first, the experience might not seem to bother the giraffe too much – but it has an immense impact in later life. Throughout their twenty-odd year lifespan, giraffes don't jump. Never. Paradoxically, the world's tallest animal is actually scared of heights. You can see this phenomenon in action in any zoo, anywhere in the world. You might expect a large animal like a giraffe to be penned in by high electric fences, but instead there are just low barriers and narrow moats separating them from the general public. Every giraffe is physically capable of jumping the moat and fence combination, but none ever does. That first terrifying bump on the head mentally conditions the giraffe into the firm impression that it's better off with four feet firmly on the ground.

The point is - we are all far guiltier than we might think of behaving like giraffes. We too are conditioned far more than we think by our earlier experiences and how we interpret them. Just when we need to change most, we may well find that we can't. We can be locked in by our past, our subconscious fears, our psychological conditioning or simply by the idea that we've always done it that way.

Powerful beliefs can take people to places that they otherwise would not go. Nelson Mandela, when in prison said, "If you want to make peace with your enemy, you have to work with your enemy. Then he becomes your partner."

A very powerful statement and a very powerful belief.

Beliefs are the essence of a person's behaviour.

The range of what we think and do is limited by what we fail to notice.

And because we fail to notice that we fail to notice there is little we can do to change until we notice how failing to notice shapes our thoughts and deeds.

R.D. Laing

BE AWARE – THINK STRATEGICALLY

Two men are running in a forest when they disturb a bear. It's that time of year when the bears are hungry and sure enough the bear comes after them. The two men run as fast as they can. But four legs are faster than two and slowly, but surely, the bear gets closer, and closer, and closer. Then, suddenly, one of the two men stops. He goes over and sits down on the edge of a log, and starts changing from his heavy trekking boots into a pair of fancy Nike running shoes.

"What are you doing?" his friend asks. *"You won't outrun the bear, even in those."*

Then very calmly, the man gets up from the log, looks at his friend, and says:

"I know. But I don't have to outrun the bear. I just have to outrun you."

How aware are you? How strategic are you in the way you think?

Have a look at the sentence below. How many F's do you see?

Finished files are the result of many years of scientific study combined with the experience of many years.

The 6F thinkers among us will see all six F's; the 3F thinkers see only 3F's because they have "tunnel vision" thinking.

Winners are 6F thinkers. They think strategically. They see the bigger picture. They think outside the box. They are aware of everything and everyone around them.

Winning is about being aware. Aware of your thoughts. Aware of your feelings. Aware of your actions. When we have better awareness we make better choices. And better choices result in better results.

Winners are 6F thinkers.

Things which matter most

must never be at the mercy of things that matter least.

Goethe

TIDY UP YOUR INCOMPLETES

We live in a world of choice. More television channels, more apps, more ways of communicating. Life is more complicated. In a hectic world with many competing interests it is easy to leave something undone as you try to embrace the many daily demands of modern lifestyle. Being a winner means getting things done.

Have you ever had a boss who would start things but never see them through? It is a frustrating experience. What frustrations do you create for others by your incompletes? Five things completed have more power than ten things not completed.

Are there areas of your life that have been left uncompleted? When you don't complete the past, you can't be free to fully embrace the present. I recently made contact with two old work colleagues with whom I had reason to disagree with in the past. I simply lifted the telephone and said that whatever had happened in the past was now over and the purpose of my call was to make contact and say hello. You can only tidy up your incompletes when your level of thinking shifts from where it was when the problem was created to where it is now.

Incompletes – whether physical or emotional – drain you. They drain all your energy. Keep in mind the saying – if an untidy desk is the sign of a cluttered mind, what is the significance of a clean desk? Have a winning mindset and keep your desk clean.

Five things completed have more power than ten things not completed.

One's real life is so often the life that one does not lead.

Oscar Wilde

DON'T LIVE SOMEONE ELSE'S DREAMS

Be true to yourself. Don't live your life through others. Don't spend your life pleasing others – going to medical school because your parents wanted you to, getting married because it is the thing to do, buying a top of the range car to keep up with the Jones' even though you can't afford it.

Always remember, "You are what you are." To express who you really are (or want to be) is a challenging and exhilarating thing to do. The gay community has the song "I Am What I Am" as their anthem. Five very powerful words. I recently spoke with someone who struggled for many years with his sexuality. He lived a lie because he was scared of being rejected. Today he is a confident and outgoing man who is very much at peace with himself. He told me he could never tell his parents he was gay as he didn't want to disappoint them or make them unhappy. When he did eventually tell them he realised that what makes them happy is knowing and seeing that he's happy.

Everyone strives for a life of fulfilment. You must never deny yourself fulfilment before you even set out on the journey of seeking fulfilment. To do so results in constantly seeking the approval of others because you are unable to approve yourself. Always put self-approval before social-approval. When you need to seek the approval of others you say and do the things others want to hear and see. You are easily influenced. You always want to be liked. You are never happy with what you have got. Enjoyment is fleeting, often superficial. Your core values and principles are often compromised when you fail to be true to yourself.

What's more important in life than being who you truly are? Fulfilment comes from living your truth. Pursuing your desires and dreams. "To thine own self be true," wrote Shakespeare. There's no point in getting to the end and realising you never let the authentic you come out to play.

Be authentic. Be you.

Your core values and principles are often compromised when you fail to be true to yourself.

The art of living is simply getting up after you've been knocked down.

It's the first principle of life.

Joe Biden

(Vice-President of The United States of America)

LIFE IS CHALLENGING

It is usually the most challenging events in our life that truly shape who we are. Challenge, conflict, confusion and uncertainty are stepping stones on the path to growth. Every setback carries the seeds of an even greater opportunity. The more painful the event, the more profound the lesson is likely to be. Pain can serve us so well if we choose to learn the lessons from it.

We learn more from the times that challenge us than we do from times of success. Walt Disney is quoted as saying, "All the adversity I've had in my life, all my troubles and obstacles, have strengthened me. You may not realise it when it happens, but a kick in the teeth may be the best thing in the world for you." Recently a colleague shared with me a moving account of a difficult family situation he had just come through. He remarked that "The difficult way is nearly over but I have learned in it lessons I could learn in no other way."

In times of success we can get caught up in shallow pursuits and pleasures. In challenging times we appreciate family, friends and the simple pleasures and beauties that are all around us. So remember, sometimes it is life's greatest challenges that present life's biggest opportunities. Challenge introduces you to your very best self. Easy times rarely make you better. They only make you complacent and take things for granted. Difficult circumstances and challenging times often create new ways in which we see the world and others in it, and what life is asking of us.

In times of challenge ask yourself one simple question - "Will this matter a year from now, or five years from now?"

If not, move on.

Sometimes it is life's greatest challenges that present life's biggest opportunities.

Mountains inspire awe in any human person who has a soul.

They remind us of our frailty, our unimportance, of the briefness of our span upon this earth.

Elizabeth Aston

LIFE IS SHORT

Every life will come to an end. We need to keep reminding ourselves that in the overall scheme of things each of us will not be here that long – no matter how long you live. I'm 53 and if I compare my life to a football match I'm in the opening ten minutes of the second half. The journey of life is short. It's a one-way ticket. There is no return fare. So we need to make the best of it.

Most of us let life act on us rather than act on life. Very few of us create something with our lives that outlives us. We all have a very short period of time in our life to make our mark. What will be your legacy? What will you do to make a difference? How can you be of significance?

I'm 53 and if I compare my life to a football match I'm in the opening ten minutes of the second half.

You need to keep your eye on the ball.

If you are a second in front or a second behind you'll miss the shot.

You have to stay in the moment.

Martina Navratilova

THE GAME OF INCHES

"You find out life's this game of inches, so is football. Because in either game – life or football – the margin for error is so small. I mean, one half step too late or too early and you don't quite make it. One half second too slow, too fast and you don't quite catch it. The inches we need are everywhere around us. They're in every break of the game, every minute, every second. On this team we fight for that inch. On this team we tear ourselves and everyone else around us to pieces for that inch. We claw with our fingernails for that inch. Because we know when we add up all those inches, that's going to make the difference between winning and losing, between living and dying."

These are the words from Al Pacino's "Inches" speech in the movie *Any Given Sunday*. Pacino plays Tony D'Amato, the coach of the Miami Sharks, a fictional National Football League team. The speech has a distinct, recurring theme – life is a game of inches.

Why is Apple one of the most profitable businesses in the world? Why is Easyjet so successful at providing low cost air travel? Why do the New Zealand All-Blacks win almost every rugby match they play? Because each of them work so hard at what they are good at in order to excel in their particular field. They never rest on their laurels. They never take success for granted. They always seek to improve, to win.

Look at a winning individual or a winning business and you'll see someone who is hard working, creative and is constantly looking for those "inches" of improvement that will make the difference. It is often the case that those who work the hardest, who discipline themselves, who give up certain pleasurable things in order to win, are usually the happiest people (or the happiest places to work in).

Life is a game of inches. Winners care about the inches. Winners do the little things that others don't value as much – and do them well.

Winners do the little things that others don't value as much – and do them well.

Perfection is not attainable, but if we chase perfection we can catch excellence.

Vince Lombardi

THE GARDEN FENCE

The story is told about the morning a young Steve Jobs was asked by his stepfather to paint their garden fence.

Jobs was just 13 at the time. The fence was rather long so he worked at a really fast pace to have the fence painted in time for his stepdad's return from work at 5 pm.

By 3 pm Steve had the fence painted inside and outside so he decided to give the outside of the fence a second coat of paint. When his stepdad returned home the young Jobs was really excited.

"Dad, I've got the whole fence painted inside and out – and I even gave the outside a second coat."

"But why did you not give the inside a second coat?" queried the stepdad.

"Sure no one will see it" said Steve.

"But we'll see it" came the reply.

It was a lesson the young Steve Jobs would later apply in business.

He told about the day an engineer approached him with a newly finished iPad. The engineer was so pleased about how neat and slick it looked. Jobs removed the back cover, and spotting a component that wasn't fitted properly he remarked, "That component is not straight."

"But sure no one will see it" retorted the engineer.

"But we'll see it" – and thereafter Jobs insisted that every engineer initial the inside of every Apple product.

But we'll see it........

People don't buy what you do; they buy why you do it.

Simon Sinek

START WITH WHY

Why is there a hole in the middle of a Polo mint?

When you know and understand your life purpose you know your "Why?"

Why do you do what you do? Why do you exist? When you can answer these questions you can unlock another of the seven core principles of winning.

In his excellent book *Start With Why*,[5] Simon Sinek explains why winners in life and business and everything else move past knowing what they do and how they do it, to ask the more important question – WHY? Sinek believes that in life and in business it doesn't matter what you do, it matters WHY you do what you do. He claims that very few people or businesses can clearly articulate WHY they do what they do. By WHY, Sinek means their purpose, their cause, or their belief. WHY does your business exist? WHY do you get out of bed every morning? And WHY should anyone care?

Sinek analyses a variety of winning individuals and winning businesses and discovers that they all think in the same way – they all started with the WHY question. It is a fascinating read.

You won't have all the answers but to be a winner you must ask all the right questions. And the most important question of all is WHY?

WHY do Apple do what they do? WHY is Facebook so popular? And WHY is there a hole in the middle of a Polo mint?

You won't have all the answers but to be a winner you must ask all the right questions.

If you know the why you can live any how.

Friedrich Nietzsche

WINNERS ANSWER "WHY"

At 7.48 pm local time on 6 July 2005, the President of the International Olympic Committee (IOC), Dr Jacques Rogge, stood at a podium in the Singapore Convention Centre with a large white envelope in his hand. Jacques Rogge was about to announce the decision as to which city had been chosen to host the 2012 Summer Olympics.

Crowded in front of the London and Paris delegations, poised to record reactions to Rogge's imminent announcement, were some 50 photographers and cameramen from the world's media. Only three of these cameramen were positioned before the British. The remaining forty-seven had their cameras trained upon their French counterparts, several of whom seemed confident enough of victory to have brought bottles of champagne into the hall with them.

Sebastian Coe, leading the London bid, knew that by answering "why" London should get the Games rather than Paris would be the secret to winning. Coe's pitch on behalf of the London bid had a compelling message:

"Today's children live in a world of conflicting messages and competing distractions. Their landscape is cluttered. Their path to Olympic sport is often obscured. But it is a world we must understand and must respond to. My heroes were Olympians. My children's heroes change by the month."

He had emphasised the problem facing the Olympic Movement, but this time, with reference to his children, he had made it personal. He ended London's pitch by again repeating the core message of the bid:

"Choose London today and you send a clear message to the youth of the world: More than ever, the Olympic Games are for you......on behalf of the youth of today, the athletes of tomorrow, and the Olympians of the future, we humbly submit the bid of London 2012."

The Paris presentation had ended with a similar appeal. But it had an entirely different orientation.

> *"Paris needs the Games.*
>
> *Paris wants the Games.*
>
> *Paris loves the Games."*

Paris's presentation wasn't about the Olympic Movement. It was about Paris. London 2012's story was the IOC's story, the athletes' story, and crucially, the children's story. It was a story that answered "Why?"

My heroes were Olympians. My children's heroes change by the month.

PRINCIPLE 3

IDENTIFY YOUR GOALS

Setting goals is the first step in turning the invisible into the visible.

Tony Robbins

WHAT ARE YOUR GOALS?

Winners are always focused. Why? Because they set goals and they focus their time around those goals. Goals give structure and purpose and, most importantly, a focus. How often have you heard someone say, "I don't have enough time to do that". It's not a lack of time that's the problem but rather a lack of direction. We all have exactly the same amount of time – 24 hours each day, every day.

Goals are healthy. Goals enable you to chase the blues away. Goals create activity and activity creates the excitement you need in order to reach your accomplishments. Achieving your goals is a realisation of your potential. However, the real value of reaching a goal lies not in the result achieved but in the journey you've walked and what it has made of you as a person.

Goal setting is incredibly important and crucial to a winning mindset. Few things focus the mind as well as articulating our thoughts and ideas into plans and then sequencing them into written goals. The very act of writing your goals increases your awareness as to what's most important. When you have better awareness you will make better choices. When you make better choices, you get better results.

Setting your goals is a statement that you refuse to be mediocre, to be ordinary. Most people go through life leading very ordinary lives, always busy but never accomplishing anything. There was a very interesting experiment carried out by the French naturalist Jean-Henri Fabre on processionary caterpillars, so named because they follow each other in a procession. Fabre lined the caterpillars around a flowerpot until they formed a never-ending circle. The caterpillars went round and round the flowerpot for twenty-four hours and then the next day and then the next. At the start of the fourth day Sabre put some pine needles into the centre of the flowerpot (that's the food of the processionary caterpillar). They kept going round and round for seven full days and seven full nights until they literally dropped dead from exhaustion and starvation. With an abundance of food less than six inches away they starved to death because they confused activity with accomplishment. So many people are busy, busy, busy but never accomplish anything – because they don't have their goals.

Setting your goals is a statement that you refuse to be mediocre, to be ordinary.

We ask ourselves "Who am I to be brilliant, gorgeous, talented, fabulous?"

Actually, who are you not to be?

Your playing small doesn't serve the world.

Marianne Williamson

BELIEF IS EVERYTHING

Being a winner is about believing in yourself (and others) when no one else does. In 2000 the Irish provincial rugby team Munster lost in the final of Europe's top rugby tournament, the Heineken Cup. There was huge disappointment at their failure, particularly among the 40,000 Munster supporters who travelled to London for the game. Two years later Munster reached the final again, and lost. The newspaper headlines labelled them the "nearly men", the "bridesmaids" and the "team who can't win finals". Munster, a province steeped in the traditions of rugby, felt it was their destiny to win the biggest prize in European club rugby. They believed. They believed they could overcome these setbacks and try again, one more time. Four years later in 2006 Munster were back in the final again.... and won. There were unbridled scenes of joy among the players and their vast army of fans at the end of the game.

Munster reached their holy grail because they had self-belief. Belief is what makes things happen. Negative belief will convince you why you will fail; positive belief will demonstrate why you will win.

People tend to think that to win we need to improve knowledge, experience, skills and qualifications. These are important but the most vital area for winning is often ignored: our own beliefs. When you believe "I can do it" the "how to do it" always follows.

Self-belief is one of the most empowering attributes to have. It is said that:

20% of our success in business will be based on our wisdom (what we know)

30% will be based on our skills (our ability to do what we know to do)

50% will be based on our being (what we believe about ourselves and others).

Munster believed. In 2008 they returned to the Heineken Cup Final to win for a second time against the French aristocrats of rugby, Toulouse. After the game their manager said "It takes a good team to win it once; it takes a great team to win it twice." Munster always believed they could be the best team in Europe.

Believe.... and you can win too!

Winning is about believing in yourself (and others) when no one else does.

Some men see things as they are and ask why. Others dream things that never were and ask why not.

George Bernard Shaw

DREAM BIG

Dream big. Big dreams attract big people and even bigger outcomes. It doesn't take any more energy to create a big dream than it does to create a little dream. Dreams happen, but only if you believe and most importantly, make them happen.

There are people who will try to talk you out of your dreams. They will call you crazy and that it can't be done. They will laugh at you and ridicule you. Be the architect of your future rather than a prisoner of those around you. Believe that what you dream is possible.

Believing is a choice. It is an attitude. Call it self-esteem, self-confidence or self-assurance, but it is a belief that you have what it takes to get what you desire that determines whether you win or lose in life, business, and everything else.

The latest brain research indicates that with enough positive self-talk and positive visualisation along with the proper training, coaching and practice, anyone can learn to do almost anything. The weekend after Munster won the 2008 Rugby Heineken Cup their out-half Jerry Flannery was quoted as saying "All week I could picture us winning... I just couldn't get that picture out of my head."

My mother couldn't drive. She started to take driving lessons at age 60. She did her driving test five times and failed on each occasion. She passed at the sixth attempt. She was 64.

Many winners will tell you they were not the most gifted in their field, but they chose to believe anything was possible. They studied, practiced and were prepared to work harder than the others and that's how they got to where they are.

Be the architect of your future rather than a prisoner of those around you.

When nothing seems to help, I go and look at a stonecutter hammering away at his rock perhaps a hundred times without as much as a crack showing in it.

Yet at the hundred and first blow it will split in two, and I know it was not that last blow that did it – but all that had gone before.

Jacob Riis

THE IMPOSSIBLE DREAM

Doctors and scientists said it was impossible. Man could not run a mile in less than 4 minutes! He would die in the foolish attempt. It was an impossible dream.

Our bone structure was wrong. Wind resistance was too great. We had inadequate lung power. Our heart could not take the strain.

Sixty years ago Roger Bannister wasn't listening. He endured thousands of monotonous laps around the same university track. Determined to shape his body and mind.

May 6th 1954 at Oxford University was viewed as simply another attempt in a history of foolish attempts to achieve the impossible dream. Yet at the end of the race the stopwatches held a different view. The results were announced. "Result of one mile...time...3 minutes...." The rest was lost in the roar of the crowd.

Roger Bannister blazed across the finishing line in a time of 3 minutes, 59.4 seconds. The impossible dream was now an event for the history books. Considered one of the greatest feats in sports history.

Forty-six days after Bannister's breakthrough a different runner broke the record again. By the end of 1957 sixteen runners had achieved the impossible.

The runners did not suddenly get "better" in those few short years. They simply began to believe. Running a mile in less than four minutes was not only possible; it had been achieved!

Many of life's barriers and obstacles come from within. We create limits for ourselves. But once those barriers are broken we realise the biggest barriers are our beliefs.

What beliefs are keeping you from achieving your dreams? Don't accept them. Don't listen to the voices of doubt. Forge ahead and you too can achieve impossible dreams.

Many of life's barriers and obstacles come from within.

The ability to triumph begins with you - always.

Oprah Winfrey

THE FROG RACE

A group of small frogs were holding a race. Their goal was to reach the top of a very high tower.

On the morning of the race all the big frogs came along to spectate. When the big frogs saw the height of the tall tower they started shouting at the little frogs:

It's not possible. You will never get to the top. The tower is too high.

But the little frogs started climbing the tower, and as they climbed the big frogs kept shouting:

It's not possible. You will never get to the top. The tower is too high.

And a couple of the little frogs fell off.

But most kept climbing, and as they climbed, the big frogs kept shouting:

You will never get to the top; the tower is too high.

And sure enough, more and more of the little frogs fell off.

Except, for one little frog, that kept climbing, and climbing, and climbing, and, all on its own, this one little frog got to the top of this very high tower.

The big frogs down on the ground were flabbergasted. They were amazed. They couldn't understand – how did this one little frog, all on its own, get to the top of this very high tower?

The winner – they discovered – was deaf.

The winner – they discovered – was deaf.

Simple doesn't always mean easy.

Seth Godin.

THE SIMPLICITY OF SIMPLE

The most powerful words in any language are the simplest words. Feel the power of "please", "thank-you", "I'm sorry", "I love you", and on your wedding day "I do."

Big businesses understand the power of simple. Nike wants us to "just do it", Apple challenges us to "think different", and BSkyB tells us to "believe in better".

So it is with the goals we set. Keep them simple. The simpler they are, the more powerful they become.

Powerful goals are SMART goals.

SMART goals are specific and stretching – because if they are not, they will be vague – and you will get vague performance.

S**M**ART goals can be measured – because what gets measured gets done.

SM**A**RT goals are achievable - because if they are not achievable, they won't happen.

SMA**R**T goals are relevant – because there should always be a reason for doing something.

And finally, SMAR**T** goals are time-bound – because then we make ourselves accountable.

Keeping our goals simple and succinct is not easy. Einstein reminded us that "if you can't explain it simply enough, you don't understand it well enough." Great point.

See yourself as a billboard. The best billboards have no more than seven words and nine syllables – because it is reckoned this is what the brain can digest in the three seconds most drivers have to read the billboard's message.

We can always make everything simpler. Those who understand this mindset - win.

Apple Macintosh. Apple Mac. Apple.

The most powerful words in any language are the simplest words.

Not all dreamers are achievers, but all achievers are dreamers.

(Neuro-Linguistic Programming — NLP - maxim)

BE IMAGINATIVE AND CREATIVE

I once attended a motivational conference and the presenter opened the morning by giving each participant a white sheet of A4 paper. In the middle of the sheet was a black dot. The presenter asked each participant to write down all that they saw on the sheet of paper.

Guess what? Every participant responded that they saw the black dot and a couple of participants said they saw a lot of white. How boring? How predictable? While everyone focused on the negativity of the small black dot no one present had the creativity to let his or her mind run free and see the rest of the page as representing:

the whiteness of a fall of snow

the peacefulness of an early morning

the calmness of a silence

Einstein said, "Imagination is more important than knowledge." Each of us has imagination – the ability to create with our minds what we cannot at present see with our eyes. Through imagination we can visualise the uncreated worlds of potential that lie within us. The mind works through pictures. Pictures affect our self-image and our self-image affects the way we think, feel, and act.

The winners in life, business, and everything else are often the most imaginative.

We often refer to such people as visionaries. The very nature of a visionary is that they see what others miss. Visionaries create a compelling vision that, in effect, is a picture of the future. Kennedy told us in 1962 that America would put a man on the moon before the end of the decade "not because it is easy, but because it is hard". In the same decade Martin Luther King told us "I have a dream" and in 2008 Barack Obama proclaimed, "Yes we can."

Vision empowers and excites us to reach for what we truly desire. Vision unlocks potential. Vision never ever focuses on the black dot. Vision always sees the bigger picture.

Be brave. Keep challenging yourself to think better, feel better and act better. People pay for originality. Set no limits on the workings of your imagination or your creativity. Be a winner.

Through imagination we can visualise the uncreated worlds of potential that lie within us.

Your victory has demonstrated that no person anywhere in the world should not dare to dream of wanting to change the world for a better place.

(Nelson Mandela congratulates Barack Obama on his 2008 presidential victory)

THERE ARE NO LIMITS

Winners do what losers don't. They set goals.

In 1950 in war-torn Japan, industry and government got together and set a goal. The Japanese said they would become the No.1 nation in the world in the production of textiles. In 1959 they accomplished their objective.

In 1960, they set another goal – to be the No.1 nation in the world in the production of steel, even though there's no iron ore or coal of any significance in Japan. An absurd goal but by the end of the 60s they had achieved it.

In 1970 the Japanese set out to be the No.1 nation in the world in the production of cars by the end of the decade. They missed it by one year. It took them until 1980.

In 1980 the Japanese proclaimed, "We are going to be the No.1 nation in the world in the production of computers and electronics." And they were by the end of the decade.

The message – you must have goals to win.

You must have goals to win.

We are what we repeatedly do. Excellence, then, is not an act, but a habit.

Aristotle

THE 21-DAY HABIT

Psychologists tell us that 90% of our behaviour is habitual. There are hundreds of things you do the same every day – the routine way you shower, brush your teeth, dress, eat breakfast, drive to work, shop at the supermarket or watch television. Over the years you have developed a set of firmly entrenched habits.

The biggest impediment to winning is inherited thinking.

Inherited thinking is doing something because you have always done it that way. It is something you have done so many times it just comes naturally to you without a second thought.

I guess you will be unsure about your answer to the next question even though it is something you have done thousands of times in your lifetime. When you join your hands which thumb is on top? Right thumb or left thumb? (*Did you know the answer without having to join your hands?*). Similarly, which arm do you put on top when you fold your arms? Both of these are examples of inherited thinking - actions that have become inherited habits that we don't even think about because we just do them.

Inherited habits are powerful factors in our lives. They can be learned and unlearned. But it isn't a quick fix. Learning or unlearning an inherited habit involves a process and a tremendous commitment.

You need the two Ds to change a habit – desire and discipline. You won't change a habit without the desire to change. You won't change a habit without the discipline to change.

Your habits determine your outcomes. Negative habits sow the seeds of negative consequences. Positive habits create positive consequences. Winners recognise the importance of positive habits and the need for the two Ds to make a habit a way of life. Research shows that if you repeat a behaviour for 21 consecutive days it will become a habit. Maybe you want to stop smoking, stop biting your nails, drink more water, go to the gym or stop eating snacks at night. When you know what it is you want or have to do and know how to do it, and, most importantly, have the desire and the discipline to do it, then, in the words of those famous American philosophers - just do it!

The biggest impediment to winning is inherited thinking.

Most of the problems in life are because of two reasons;
we act without thinking or we keep thinking without acting.

Jose Sanchez

A REASON TO ACT

The word "motivation" is really a shortened version of two words – motive and action. Motivation, in its purest form, is giving ourselves, or others, a reason or a motive to act. People do things for a reason, always. Unless you have a reason to act, you won't act.

Every goal you set should be underpinned by a reason. The reason is your motive, your driver, and your measure of success. Without a reason, there is no motivation, no driver, and no measure of success.

Why are you reading this page just now? Is it because you are bored? Is it because you want to find out about how to set goals? Or is it because you loved the title of this book, can't leave it down, and are now on this page? Because there is always a reason.

When you understand the reason or reasons for your goals then you will know the purpose of your goals. This, too, is true of change. When we want to change something we must understand the reasons for changing, or we won't change.

The more definitive your reasons for acting the more likely you are to act. Clarity precedes focus and always influences outcomes.

Speaking in South California on 9 December 2007 Barack Obama delivered one of the most inspirational speeches of the new millennium. He was sowing the seeds for an announcement he would make just a few weeks later that he would run for the presidency of the United States of America. His rallying call at the end of a wonderful speech was a call to action:

One voice can change a room, and if one voice can change a room, then it can change a city, and if it can change a city, it can change a state, and if it change a state, it can change a nation, and if it can change a nation, it can change the world. Your voice can change the world.

Those last six words – how motivating. It was Obama's rallying call to action - make me your president and you and I together we will change the world.

What a powerful reason to act!

People do things for a reason, always.

When there is genuine vision, people excel and learn, not because they are told to, but because they want to.

Peter Senge

TEN QUESTIONS TO ASK YOURSELF

1. **Are your goals written down?** Writing your goals down is a magical act. It makes them real. It clarifies them, and helps bring definition and accountability to them.

2. **Are they *your* goals?** Before you embark on your goals, make sure they are truly your own.

3. **Do your goals have a deadline?** Goals without deadlines are like a race without a finishing line.

4. **What is the cost of your goals and are you willing to pay it?** Every goal has a cost – whether it is time, money or sweat. Make sure you are willing to pay the price to achieve your goal.

5. **What help will you need to accomplish your goals?** Truly great goals often require us to go beyond ourselves. Every winner learned from someone else. Success leaves clues.

6. **Are you focused on your goals?** Many people fall into the trap of unfocused goals. Or they have too many goals. You must have laser focus on your big goal.

7. **Are your goals adaptable?** Life changes. So your goals must be adaptable. This is not to be used as an excuse at the first sign of difficulty. Adaptable goals change, instead of break.

8. **Are your goals stretching?** If your goal is to do something you have already done before, then you will get the same results. Your goals should stretch your abilities.

9. **Do you believe in your goals?** More than anyone else, you have to believe in your goals. There will be critics, doubters, and people who want to see you fail. Don't listen to them. Listen to the inner voice that drives you.

10. **What did you do *today* about your goals?** You must act on your goals every single day. It is not an optional activity. If you truly have the desire and the discipline to reach your goals, you will not only think, but act on them every single day.

Success leaves clues.

.

PRINCIPLE 4

AFFIRM YOURSELF AND OTHERS OFTEN

I've learned that people will forget what you said, people will forget how you said it,

but people will never forget how you made them feel.

Maya Angelou

AFFIRM YOURSELF TO AFFIRM OTHERS

The prime need of every human being (and most organisations) is to be loved, valued and respected. All teaching starts with yourself. Do you love yourself? Do you value yourself? Do you respect yourself? When you answer yes to each of these questions you can truly affirm yourself, and in turn, affirm others. Winning means affirming yourself and others, and doing so often. Each of us likes to be affirmed. We feel good as a result of being affirmed. It could be a simple statement like "Well done" or "I am pleased with you". An affirmation may come in the form of a thank-you card for something you've done or your boss giving you Friday afternoon off in recognition of a good week's work.

When you affirm, you are thinking and acting positively. Positive thinking is a habit. We can practice it every day until it becomes second nature to us. William Shakespeare said that there is nothing either good or bad, but thinking makes it so. Our thinking influences our feelings, our words and ultimately, our actions. Are you a positive thinker? Here are the eight common qualities of positive thinkers on which to base your judgement:

Do you:

- have confidence in yourself?
- have a very strong sense of purpose?
- never have excuses for not doing something?
- never consider the idea of failing?
- work extremely hard towards your goals?
- understand your weaknesses as well as your strong points?
- accept and benefit from criticism?
- know when to defend what you are doing?

The prime need of every human being (and most organisations) is to be loved, valued and respected.

If you think you are too small to have an impact,

try going to bed with a mosquito in the room.

Anita Roddick

BE POSITIVE

Most people in life are negative. Why? Because it is the easy option.

The main reason why most people don't have a positive attitude is because it is easier to be negative. In fact, it takes no effort whatsoever to conform to "normal".

Being positive is not easy. It is considerably more challenging to be upbeat, happy, and positive – all the time. And because it's hard work and it takes practice, most people simply can't be bothered.

Your positive thinking will allow others to think positively. Your positive thinking will allow others to feel good about themselves. When you walk into a room do you turn on the lights? Do you light the place up? Do you put a smile on people's faces? Do you challenge others and help them to grow? Or when you leave, are people glad to see the back of you?

Positive people choose to be positive.

Think like a winner and flip your thinking so that:

- *I can't do that* becomes **I can do that**

- *I'm not good enough* becomes **I am good enough**

- *I'm too fat/skinny/short/tall* becomes **I like myself for who I am**

- *It will never work* becomes **this will work**

- *They aren't good enough* becomes **they are good enough.**

When we focus on negatives we exaggerate the outcome, we expect the worst, we think in absolutes, we blame, we argue from a "yes, but" stance.

As Wayne Dyer, the American author said, "Change the way you look at things, and the things you look at will change."

Change today. Think like a winner.

Be positive about life and life will be positive to you.

Be positive about life and life will be positive to you.

There is very little difference in people, but that little difference makes a big difference.

The little difference is attitude. The big difference is whether it is positive or negative.

W. Clement Stone

A 100% ATTITUDE

What does it mean to give 100%?

What makes up 100% in life?

Here's a little mathematical formula that will help you answer these questions.

If A B C D E F G H I J K L M N O P Q R S T U V W X Y Z is represented by 1 2 3 4 5 6 7 8 9 10 11 12 13 14 15 16 17 18 19 20 21 22 23 24 25 26, then:

K-N-O-W-L-E-D-G-E = 11+14+15+23+12+5+4+7+5 = 96%, and

H-A-R-D-W-O-R-K = 8+1+18+4+23+15+18+11 = 98%, but,

A-T-T-I-T-U-D-E = 1+20+20+9+20+21+4+5 = 100%.

Attitude is everything.

Attitude is more important than facts. It is more important than the past, than what other people think, or say, or do. It is more important than appearance, giftedness, or skill.

We have a choice every day regarding the attitude we will embrace for that day. When we get out of bed each morning we choose what to wear, what to have for breakfast, what to do that day. We also choose our attitude.

To be a winner – in life, business, and everything else – ATTITUDE is all-important.

Attitude is everything.

People come for what they see.

They return for how they are made to feel.

Danny Myers (New York restaurant owner)

MAKE OTHERS FEEL GOOD

People work best when they feel good about themselves.

The story is told of the occasion when Coco Chanel, the famous fashion designer, was asked how did she judge the success of her dresses. Chanel responded by saying that "If a man walks into a room and walks over to a lady wearing one of my dresses and says, "That dress looks fabulous" then Chanel said, "I have failed as a designer." But if a man walks into a room and goes over to a lady wearing one of my dresses and says, "You look fabulous" then "I have succeeded as a designer." People never forget how you make them feel.

One of the most influential personal development books ever written is Dale Carnegie's *How to Win Friends and Influence People*[6]. It has sold more than 15 million copies across the world. Written in 1936, the book is as relevant today as it ever was. At the heart of the book are Carnegie's thirty human relations principles – a set of statements that are so beautifully simple and yet profound. Here are five of the most powerful principles.

While the principles are in no particular order Principle 1 (*Don't criticise, condemn or complain*) is one of the most challenging. Interestingly Carnegie doesn't say, "Never criticise, condemn or complain" because that is just not possible. He challenges us to avoid criticising, condemning or complaining.

Dale Carnegie encourages us in Principle 4 to *become genuinely interested in other people*. Winners are always interested in people because you can't motivate someone you don't know and understand.

Carnegie's fifth principle simply encourages us to *smile*. Remember a smile can make or break a conversation, and it can make or break a relationship.

Principle 6 reminds us *that a person's name is to that person the sweetest and most important sound in any language.* We build trust when we use a person's name – and trust is the highest form of human motivation. We gain respect. Often we gain acceptance. Think of the impact when we get a person's name wrong. Or spell it wrong.

Principle 8 encourages us to *talk in terms of the other person's interests*. We all love to talk about ourselves. Research shows that the most used word in telephone conversations is "I". So, rather than talking about ourselves, encourage others to talk about themselves. Winners always do.

Trust is the highest form of human motivation.

Judge a man by his questions rather than his answers.

Voltaire

THE BRIGHT YOUNG PSYCHOLOGIST

We all like the idea of being thought of as an interesting person. Traditional thinking dictates that if you want to be considered interesting, you first need to be well read, bright, articulate, charming and witty. Well, before you subscribe to that thinking, read this:

A bright young psychologist took a month out from his normal work and flew back and forth every day from Los Angeles to New York. He would always sit in the middle seat of three.

After take-off he would start a conversation with the person either side but, rather than trying to be interesting, he would focus instead on being interested. All he did was ask great questions and let the other person speak.

At the end of the journey he would ask for their details on the premise that he could do something for them or that they would stay in touch. One week later a researcher would call the people he had sat next to. They all remembered him. They all said how much they liked him; although none could recall if he was married, or what he did for a living or where he was from (because he never told them).

However the most amazing part of the research was the fact that over 70% described him as one of the most interesting people they had EVER met!

The moral of the story – be interested rather than trying to be interesting if you want to be thought of as an interesting person.

Be interested rather than trying to be interesting if you want to be thought of as an interesting person.

Success is not the key to happiness. Happiness is the key to success.

If you love what you are doing, you will be successful.

Albert Schweitzer

TEN WAYS TO BE UNHAPPY

You can be unhappy if you make the choice to do so.

Every day you make lots of choices: what to wear, what to eat, what to do. You also make a choice about how you feel – and how you feel influences how you act. Feel happy and you will be happy. Feel unhappy and you will be unhappy. Simple, but true. Here's ten ways to be unhappy.

1. Make things bother you. Don't just let them; make them.
2. Lose your perspective on things and keep it lost; don't put first things first.
3. Find yourself a good worry, one about which you cannot do anything.
4. Be a perfectionist, which means not that you work hard to do your best, but that you condemn yourself and others for not achieving perfection.
5. Be right. Be always right. Be the only one who is always right, and be rigid in your rightness.
6. Don't trust or believe people, or accept them at anything but their worst and weakest.
7. Be suspicious. Insist that others have hidden motives.
8. Always compare yourself unfavourably to others.
9. Take personally everything that happens to you.
10. Don't give yourself wholeheartedly to anyone or anything.

You can be unhappy if you make the choice to do so.

The mind is its own place and in itself can make a heaven of hell, a hell of heaven.

John Milton

MINDSET MATTERS

On Monday 30 April 2007 the smoking ban in public places was introduced in the UK and a way of life changed forever. The days when it was fashionable to smoke in the office, with everyone lighting up together in team meetings, sharing camaraderie in the fog of smoke, were gone forever. Such behaviour, previously accepted as the norm, was preposterous and no longer to be tolerated. So what happened? The mindset around smoking changed. While this behavioural change was brought about by changes in the law, it also happened because of the commitment of people convinced and determined to stop passive smoke damaging their health.

Look at the last three letters of the word mindset. Are you set in a particular way of thinking? Do you limit your ambitions? Do you think negatively? Do you always hold back from asking that one important question, making that one important call or taking that one decisive step? When you do, you give all your power away.

Be open-minded, because you become what you think. The actions you take each day create your outcomes. And since every action you take is preceded by a thought, what you think drives what happens to you. Think people are good and you go through your days with an open heart. Think you deserve the best and your actions will reflect that thinking. Think powerfully. Expect to win and such thinking will shape your outcomes.

Mindset matters.

Look at the last three letters of the word mindset. Are you set in a particular way of thinking?

Two men looked out the same prison bars.

One saw the dirt on the road; the other saw the beauty of the stars.

Frederick Langbridge

VISUALISE WHAT YOU WANT

In 1995 I began building my own house. For the previous two years I had a picture in my mind of my dream house. I visualised what the kitchen would look like and the master bedroom. I drew sketches of the front door and the shape of the driveway and the garden. I drove 150 miles to take a picture of windows I had seen in a house while on holiday a few years earlier. Visualising what you want is a great way to get what you want. Today I have my dream house.

Sports athletes often use the power of visualisation. Sally Gunnell, the Olympic Hurdles Champion, would visualise running her race hundreds of times a day in the months leading up to her next race. When Jonny Wilkinson was asked about how nervous he felt as he attempted the drop kick goal in the last minute of extra-time that won the Rugby World Cup for England in 2003 he replied, "I wasn't nervous because I had pictured that moment hundreds of times in my mind." When NASA was working on putting a man on the moon they had a huge picture of the moon covering the entire wall from floor to ceiling in their main working area. Everyone was clear on the goal and they reached that goal two years ahead of schedule.

Liverpool Football Club have won the Champions League (formerly the European Cup) five times. They were the dominant force in European football in the 80s. When visiting teams walk out to play at Liverpool they are met by a sign at the top of a set of steps that reads "This Is Anfield". It is a clever way of creating a picture of fear and invincibility on the part of Liverpool in the minds of visiting teams.

We should never underestimate the power of visualising what it is we want as a key step in getting what we want.

We should never underestimate the power of visualising what it is we want as a key step in getting what we want.

Worry does not empty tomorrow of its sorrow.

It empties today of its strength.

Corrie Ten Boom

WORRY SAPS YOUR ENERGY

It is said that 90% of what we worry about never happens.

Think back to this day last week. Can you recall five things you did that day? Probably not. Many people spend so much time worrying about things they have to do, yet a couple of days later those things that seemed so important then have now disappeared from their radar.

There are two days in every week about which we should not worry – yesterday and tomorrow. Yesterday has passed forever beyond our control. We cannot undo a single act we performed or a single word we said. Tomorrow's sun will rise, either in splendour or behind a mask of clouds, but it will rise. Tomorrow is a new day. Until it does, we have no stake in tomorrow, for it is yet to be born. This leaves only one day – today. Every day each of us gets a fresh set of 24 hours. Not everyone gets one. Make the best of today.

Worry saps your energy. It tires you. It stresses you. Too many people worry about too many insignificant things. Here's the litmus test. If there is something you have to do, ask yourself – what will be the consequences if I don't do it? If it is something important it will have consequences. If it is not important it won't have consequences. Winners don't worry about unimportant things and they don't worry about important things either. They just get the important things done. That's why winners are usually the best organised, the most energetic and good to be around.

If your thinking is to dwell on bad experiences and to worry over things you cannot change, it's a waste of your time and energy. If your intention is to reflect on the lessons that events have taught you, that's a positive thing. You are letting your past inform you and make you wiser and better. What's the point in regretting things you've done and cannot be changed? If you do, you probably drain so much of your energy you lose the enjoyment that comes with accomplishing your important tasks.

90% of what we worry about never happens.

Teach us delight in simple things.

Rudyard Kipling

ENJOY THE SIMPLE THINGS IN LIFE

There's a lovely saying, "Success comes from simplicity." The phone company O2 must have had this in mind when they introduced a tariff for their pay and go phones and simply called it "Simplicity." It was one of their biggest-ever selling tariffs.

Sometimes it can be the most simple of touches that can have the greatest impact. I vividly recall one moment from the funeral of Pope John Paul 11 in April 2005. Amidst the great pomp and ceremony of the occasion there suddenly appeared the Pope's coffin – a plain wooden box.

Some of life's best pleasures are its simplest ones. My father is 87 and thankfully is in great health. He has, and still does, lead a very simple life. He whiles away his day in his vegetable garden and faithfully visits his local pub every night of the week for a whiskey and a bottle of stout. He also manages to squeeze in one night of bingo into his weekly schedule. Life for him is about simplicity. He summed it up perfectly when he once said "There is nothing to beat an ordinary day."

Training your brain to appreciate the little things in life sets you up to embrace and honour the big things in life.

Winning does come from the simple things in life. All my learning has come from two key sources – life experiences and reading books. Reading books – a simple activity for me – shapes my thinking and forms my personal philosophy.

Make time to read. The readers of today are the winners of tomorrow.

Sometimes it can be the most simple of touches that can have the greatest impact.

You know, there are two good things in life – freedom of thought and freedom of action.

W. Somerset Maugham

THE BEST THINGS IN LIFE

There's a song called *Money* by The Beatles with the opening line "The best things in life are free."

What's your "best things" list? How about these for starters?

1. Hearing your favourite song on the radio
2. Lying in bed listening to the rain outside
3. Walking in your bare feet on the beach
4. Finding the sweater you want is on sale for half price
5. Accidentally overhearing someone say something nice about you
6. Hot chocolate
7. Finding a £20 note in your coat from last winter
8. Waking up and realising you still have a few hours left to sleep
9. Butterflies in your stomach every time you see that one person
10. Having someone play with your hair
11. Getting into bed with freshly washed sheets
12. Driving the car with the window down on a sunny day.

The best things in life are free.

PRINCIPLE 5

KNOW WHAT YOU EXCEL AT AND DO IT!

The final forming of a person's character lies in their own hands.

Anne Frank

WHAT'S YOUR VOCATION IN LIFE?

An old mentor once gave me a most valuable piece of advice. He said, "Don't start out in life looking to make money. Too many people make that mistake. Do what you know you have a talent for doing and, if you are good enough at it, the money will come." How right he was.

Years ago when my eldest sister got married, my new brother-in-law, who was a plumber by profession, told me that one day he would own a chain of nightclubs. He went to live in Canada for two years after getting married and worked as a plumber during the day and a gardener in the evenings to build up a sound financial base. He returned home and set up his own coal delivery business. Eight years later he sold the coal business and applied for planning permission to turn an old schoolhouse in his local village into a nightclub. He was turned down. Instead he bought an old run-down pub in a village some forty miles away, travelled there to work every day for two years and then sold it on as a flourishing business. He reapplied for planning permission for a nightclub on a green field site in his home village and was successful this time. He worked in the nightclub for two years and then leased it out. He then bought a second nightclub, leased it out and has since added a third nightclub to his portfolio. When I asked him recently what was the secret to his success he replied, "Hard work – and I love what I do."

Jack Welch said, "Determine your own destiny or someone else will." How true. There is something powerful about being and living who you are because you are the only person who can play that role. Authenticity is the ability to discover your own motivations and your hidden strengths and then to find the work and personal situations that allow you to fly - to feel fulfilled and "alive".

The biggest mistake people make in life is not trying to make a living doing what they most enjoy. The winners in life, business, and everything else focus entirely on what they excel at and delegate or empower others to do the rest. This means they have the time to do what they love doing. Many people die with their music still in them, still unplayed. Live life to the full, be the best you can be, and let your music play!

Many people die with their music still in them, still unplayed.

It's the possibility of having a dream come true that makes life interesting.

Paulo Coelho

SEIZE THE WINDOWS OF OPPORTUNITY

From time to time life throws each of us little glimpses of opportunity.

The difference between winning and losing can come down to how swiftly you respond to the windows of opportunity that show up - your destiny is ultimately defined by how you respond to such opportunities.

Don't let these opportunities pass you by. A part of life is about key moments and that includes the opportunities you create for yourself. As a young boy my dream was to attend the F.A. Cup Final. I did so in 1995. As a teenager I watched Wimbledon every summer and dreamed of sitting in the sun watching the great tennis players while eating strawberries and cream. I did so in 1996 and saw Martina Navratilova play. I have met and shook hands with the late Pope John Paul II and with the Queen. These were opportunities that came my way and I grasped them with both hands. In years to come I will always remember these occasions with fondness.

What are your windows of opportunity? Swimming with dolphins, visiting one of the wonders of the world or simply spending quality time with your loved ones? Winners champion their highest potential and aim to go where others don't dare. They don't think small.

Think big and your life will be full of opportunities that will not pass you by.

Winners champion their highest potential and aim to go where others don't dare.

The talent of success is nothing more than doing what you can do, well.

Henry W. Longfellow

WHEN DO YOU PERFORM AT YOUR BEST?

The Irish golfer Rory McIlroy says he gets his best ideas when he is not on the golf course. Many of the top people in the top organisations will tell you the same. Few people get their best ideas at work. I get my best ideas when I've switched off from work – when I'm relaxed and enjoying myself. It might be when I'm having a swim, or on a long walk, or sitting over a coffee reading a good book. What I've learned is that spending all your time working will not make you more productive and certainly not more creative. In his autobiography *My Life,* Bill Clinton claims that every significant mistake he ever made in his life - both personal and political - he made when he was too tired.

I got the idea for this book when I was on a treadmill in the gym. That's a time when I feel relaxed and when my mind is most creative. Creativity comes when you are relaxed, happy and enjoying the moment.

I am also at my most creative first thing in the morning and when I've had a sound sleep. I do most of my writing then. I try to set aside one hour each morning to collate my thoughts and put them in print. This is the time when I know I'm at my best – my peak performing time.

When is your peak performance time? When is your mind most creative? The best and most creative people identify their peak performance times and then use this time to optimise their creative talents. Paul McCartney wasn't sitting in a big studio with lots of lights and recording equipment when he came up with the lyrics for *Mull of Kintyre.* I don't think I need to tell you where he was.

Few people get their best ideas at work.

Everyone thinks of changing the world,
but no one thinks of changing himself.

Leo Tolstoy

WHAT ARE YOUR BEST PRACTICES?

Practice is the price a winner pays to be called a winner. What are your best practices?

Here's my personal top 10:

1. Three long walks a week around my local park (I don't particularly like going to the gym but when I do I never regret it afterwards).

2. A good night's sleep (I need a minimum of 8 hours – I could never survive on the 3-4 hours sleep that Margaret Thatcher survived on),

3. Make use of quality thinking time:

> -first thing in the morning

> -on the treadmill

> -when I'm driving in my car

4. Massage (once a month)

5. Good diet

6. Record my thoughts (on my iPhone – I may even jump out of bed in the middle of the night to record a thought).

7. Plan my day (a closed "To Do" list with a maximum of six things on it).

8. Always do the most difficult thing first.

9. Read widely (the great autobiographies).

10. Seek out interesting people.

Practice is the price a winner pays to be called a winner.

The expert in everything was once a beginner.

President Rutherford B. Hayes

ACT AS IF YOU HAVE ALREADY ACHIEVED YOUR GOAL

How would you act if you were already a top salesman, a highly paid consultant, a world-class athlete, a much sought after motivational speaker, a best-selling author or a celebrated musician? How would you think, talk, act, carry yourself, dress, eat, travel or treat other people? And, how would others treat you?

It is often said, "Your job defines you." Maybe so, maybe not - but it certainly influences how others perceive you and, in turn, relate to you.

How do winners act? They exude self-confidence, ask for what they want, and say what they don't want. They think anything is possible; they take risks and celebrate their successes.

In his book *The Secrets of Success at Work*[7] Richard Hall says:

You don't just have to walk like a manager, you must also think like a manager if you want to get on - and not just think like one but also look as if you are thinking.

Do you think like a winner because when you think like a winner you will act like a winner?

Do you think like a winner because when you think like a winner you will act like a winner?

Be so good they can't ignore you.

Steve Martin

JUST DO IT!

To be a winner you have to do what winners do and winners are doers. They are action-orientated. They learn from experience and improve through feedback and, as a result, become more efficient and effective at what they do.

If you want to win in life, business, and everything else you must take action. At one of my seminars I light a candle and ask all of the participants to stare at the candle together intently for thirty seconds to watch the flame go out. Of course it never does, until I go over and blow it out. Without action, nothing happens.

Some people spend their whole lives waiting for the perfect time to do something. There's rarely a perfect time to do anything. What is important is to just get started. Get into the game. Get on the playing field.

Many people fail to take action because they are afraid to fail. Winners realise that mistakes are opportunities for learning and failure is an important part of the learning process. Not only do we need to stop being so afraid of failure but we also need to be willing to fail. There can be no success without failure.

Most start-up businesses fail. However, if the founding entrepreneur is 55 years or older, statistics show that the business has a 75% better chance of survival. These older entrepreneurs have already learned from their mistakes. In a lifetime of learning from their failures they have developed a knowledge base and the skills and self-confidence that better enables them to overcome the obstacles to winning.

Mistakes are opportunities for learning and failure is an important part of the learning process.

Things which matter most must never be at the mercy of things which matter least.

Goethe

AN INTERVIEW WITH AN OLD WOMAN

"You've lived a long life," I said.

"Yes" came the old woman's reply. "And life has taught me many lessons."

"Would you share them with me?" I asked.

"Sure" said the old woman.

"What surprises me most about mankind is that they get bored with childhood, they rush to grow up, and then they long to be children again. They lose their health to make money, and then lose their money to restore their health.

By thinking anxiously about the future, they forget the present, such that they live in neither the present nor the future. They live as if they will never die, and die as though they had never lived."

"Are there any of life's lessons you'd want me to learn?" I asked.

"Oh yes" she replied.

"Learn that you cannot make anyone love you.

All that you can do is let yourself be loved.

Learn that it is not good to compare yourself to others.

Learn to forgive by practicing forgiveness.

Learn that it only takes a few seconds to open profound wounds in those you love and it can take many years to heal them.

Learn that a rich man is not one who has the most,

but is one who needs the least.

Learn that there are people who love you dearly but simply do not yet know how to express or show their feelings.

And finally, try your best, give of your best, and above all, be your best."

Life has taught me many lessons.

If you are going to achieve excellence in big things, you develop the habit in little matters. Excellence is not an exception; it is a prevailing attitude.

Colin Powell

GET THE FUNDAMENTALS RIGHT

The story is told that the legendary American football coach Vince Lombardi had a routine he religiously performed on the first day of training each season. He would hold up a football, show it to the players who had been playing the sport for many years and say, "Gentlemen, ...this is a football!" He talked about its size and shape, how it can be kicked, carried or passed. He took the team out on to the empty field and said, "This is a football field." He walked them around the field, describing the dimensions, the shape, the rules, and how the game is played.

Lombardi knew that even these experienced players, and indeed the team, could become great only by mastering the fundamentals. They could spend their time mastering the intricate trick plays but until they mastered the fundamentals of the game, they would never become a great team.

Look at the most successful businesses, the great artists, the best leaders, and all of them have mastered the fundamentals. The current Barcelona football team have been credited as being one of the greatest club sides in the world. Under their coach Pep Guardiola they developed a style of play based around two fundamental beliefs – you must keep possession of the ball at all times and when you lose possession you have five seconds to win it back. It was a very simple and hugely successful philosophy,

It's easy to overlook the fundamentals. When Ford produced the first motor car they forgot to include a reverse gear. When astronauts Neil Armstrong and Buzz Aldrin walked on to the moon on 20 July 1969 they had to be careful not to close the spaceship's door behind them – NASA had forgotten to put a door handle on the outside of the craft.

When we know the ABC of what we do, how we do it, and why we do it, the rest is fun.

Winners do the fundamentals right.

It's easy to overlook the fundamentals.

Life consists not in holding good cards but in playing those you hold well.

Josh Billings

WORKING TO LIVE OR WORKING FOR LOVE?

We all have to work for a living – in some way. The hen has to lay eggs, a cow has to give milk, and a canary has to sing.

But are you working to live or working for love? When you love what you do, you'll love what you do.

I remember going to visit a tile shop. It was 5.20 pm. I reckoned I would have little more than ten minutes to decide on the type of tile I wanted. I dashed in the shop door and asked the burly shop assistant standing behind the counter "What time do you close at?"

"We close when you're happy." What a super response!

When you give people what they want in a way they least expect then you are on to a winner. I have been back to that shop on several occasions since and have always bought on every visit.

We live in an uncertain world. The new life skill today is the ability to deal with uncertainty. Young people today don't want a job for life. They want a job with life.

When you are passionate about what you do, that passion will shine through. It is said that the definition of passion is that you don't see the time passing. Look at the winners in life and you will see a passionate person loving what they do.

Do you love what you do?

When you give people what they want in a way they least expect then you are on to a winner.

When was the last time you did something for the first time?

(Emirates Airlines ad)

DO SOMETHING FOR THE FIRST TIME

We crave routine. It's just the way we are. It's a survival thing. It's so easy to eat the same breakfast each day, to visit the same hair stylist, to do the same things at work each day. We get stuck in a rut and while it is easy to get into a rut, it is never easy to get out.

Why is routine so important to us? Because we need certainty and anything less makes us uncomfortable. But winning is about getting good at being uncomfortable. Winning is about trying new things. Because so many of us fall into routine, we take things for granted, we accept things as they are, we play small with our lives, we stop taking risks, we stop aiming for the mountaintop.

I lived in a small village at the foot of a great mountain for almost all my childhood. The saying "Those who live nearest the mountain are the last to climb it" is very apt here. People came from far and wide to climb that mountain. I never did, until recently.

When was the last time you did something for the first time? Do something new – today!

Winning is about getting good at being uncomfortable.

I'm not a businessman. I'm a business, man!

Jay-Z

YOU ARE A BRAND

You are a brand. You mightn't think so, but when people hear your name they conjure up some association. When people see you, they will respond in a certain way. Like it or not, you are a brand.

A brand is a promise.

Jeff Bezos, founder of Amazon, believes "Your brand is what people say about you when you are not in the room." Brilliant!

The big brands know what they stand for — think Kellogg's or Heinz. Brands are consistent. They never let you down. Brands are worth paying a bit more for, not least because they work hard to maintain their reputation and to deliver. Brands stand for something — think Anita Roddick and The Body Shop. Brands ooze personality. People talk about them. They have attitude. They speak their own voice. Brands are widely known. They are attractive, often tempting.

Your brand is not just how you look; it's what you are, what you represent and what you believe.

What's your brand then? Does your brand shout "cutting edge" "distinctive" "with it" "cool" "unique"?

Be a brand. Be a winning brand.

Your brand is not just how you look, it's what you are, what you represent and what you believe.

PRINCIPLE 6

SURROUND YOURSELF WITH POSITIVE PEOPLE

If you're the smartest one of your friends, you need new friends.

Dennis Kimbro

SEEK OUT ENERGY CREATORS

Take a moment to think about the people you spend most time with – at work, at home or in your hobbies or social life.

Are they people who stress you out? Do they speak the language of negativity – I couldn't, I can't, maybe, what if? Do they waste time needlessly with idle gossip and small talk? Do they kill the conversation when they walk into the room? Are they are always busy but never get anything done?

They are energy sappers.

Are they just bland and boring? Do they never inspire you to go out of your way to connect with them? Do they seldom make conversation and leave you to initiate all the discussion? Do they rarely offer anything of true and lasting value? Do they just about exist?

They are energy neutrals.

Or are they enthusiastic, energetic, passionate, happy people? Are they interesting to talk to? Are they open to change, to learn? Do they put a smile on your face? Do they enjoy life?

They are energy creators.

Surround yourself with energy creators. Tolerate energy neutrals. Avoid energy sappers.

It is said that you are the average of the five people you spend the most time with. We will fly as high or as low as the people we associate with.

Here's an interesting exercise. Think of the five people (adults) you spend most time with. How many of them are energy creators?

We become like the people we spend most time with. If you want to be a winner, you have to start hanging out with winners. Winning is contagious. So is losing. Free yourself from the negative influences of energy sappers. Hang out with people who are happy, who are growing, who want to learn, who don't mind saying sorry or thank you and, above all, help you grow too. Such people will bring out a winning mindset in you!

It is said that you are the average of the five people you spend the most time with.

Instead of worrying about what people say of you, why not spend time trying to accomplish something they will admire.

Dale Carnegie

DON'T WORRY WHAT OTHERS THINK OR SAY ABOUT YOU

The title above sounds like a glib remark. "Of course I worry about what others think or say about me" I hear you shout. Well don't. I always remember a story I heard at one of my college psychology lectures. Dr. Daniel Amen calls it the 18/40/60 rule. When you're 18 you worry about what everybody is thinking about you; when you're 40, you don't much care about what anybody thinks about you; when you're 60, you realise nobody's been thinking about you anyway.

Big surprise – nobody's thinking about you anyway! They are too busy worrying about their own problems and if they are thinking about you at all, they are wondering what you are thinking about them. Key point – people think about themselves, not you.

The time you waste worrying about what other people think or say about you could be better spent on thinking about and doing the things that are important to you. The reality is that it doesn't matter what other people think or say about you. All that matters is what *you* think of you. We waste so much energy worrying about others' opinions, wanting to be liked and needing to please. Winning in life, business, and everything else is about rising above social approval – to self-approval. Respect you. When you are running your own race and playing your own game why worry what anyone else thinks or feels or says about you? Self-approval is not about being liked or being popular. What matters most is being true to yourself.

You can only define yourself from within and when you do so, you will care less about what others think or say about you. You will care more about what others think of themselves, including their relationship with you. You'll no longer build your emotional life on other people's weaknesses.

Winners build their lives on their strengths.

Winning is about rising above social approval – to self-approval.

You cannot do a kindness too soon, for you never know how soon it will be too late.

Ralph Waldo Emerson

ACT OF KINDNESS

John was in hospital. He was now an old man, paralysed from the waist down and bedridden. He shared a ward with five other men. John's bed was located beside the door into the ward. He could hear and often see all the activity going on daily in the corridor but he was removed from seeing what was going on in the world outside. In the bed at the back of the ward was Joe, another elderly man. Joe's bed was next to a large window. Each morning after the nurse pulled open the blinds John would ask the same question:

"What's it like outside today Joe?"

"It is sunny today John. There's a little rabbit on the lawn and there's a trail in the sky from a passing plane. It's a beautiful day."

Every morning John asked Joe the same question and faithfully Joe described the scene outside. John enjoyed Joe's eloquent descriptions and attention to detail.

One morning the nurse arrived as normal. She pulled open the blinds. John asked Joe his usual question. There was no reply.

"Joe's gone." said the nurse.

"Gone?" asked John.

"Yes. He passed away during the night."

There was silence.

Walking towards John's bed the nurse spotted a tear in John's eye.

"Joe was a wonderful man," she said. "Of all the patients in here I don't think I ever met his like. He was in great pain and never ever complained."

"I know." said John, "I will miss him. Every morning, without fail, he described for me the scene outside that big window. He was my window to the world."

"Joe was blind," said the nurse. "He didn't see anything out that big window."

Be like Joe. Think of others. In helping others be happy we can be happy ourselves.

In helping others be happy we can be happy ourselves.

Respect commands itself and it can neither be given nor withheld when it is due.

Eldridge Cleaver

SHOW RESPECT

Treat people with respect – always. To get respect, show respect.

There is a lovely story about the highly respected consultant who was hired at great cost to reveal his many years of wisdom with the management team of a large pharmaceutical company. The consultant walked into the conference room and looked intensely at the assembled group. He then reached for his marker and wrote four words on the flipchart beside him – "treat people with respect". He smiled at his audience. And then he left.

When people feel respected they feel better about themselves. People who feel good, do good. Reflect for a moment on this question. Which is greater – power or respect? Many leading personalities (and organisations) who have had to deal with any type of public humiliation will tell you that losing respect is always more difficult. Respect is priceless.

Good manners show those around you that you care about them. Good manners show people that you respect them.

To get respect, show respect.

Little things matter.

Aviva Insurance strapline

DO THE LITTLE THINGS OTHERS DON'T VALUE AS MUCH – AND DO THEM WELL

Little things matter. Too often we underestimate the power of a touch, a smile, a kind word, a listening ear, an honest compliment or the smallest act of caring. Put your hand gently on someone's shoulder in his or her time of need and you'll help lift a huge weight with a simple touch. There are hundreds of languages in the world but one smile speaks them all.

The winners in life, business, and everything else are always pursuing, or doing that one little thing, or things, to make the difference. What are these little things? Do they pay off?

Sport at the highest level gives us some great examples of doing the little things that often make the difference. When Sir Clive Woodward managed England to their first and only Rugby World Cup triumph in 2003 he put a great emphasis on what he called the "critical non-essentials", the little things that make the difference between winning and losing. In his excellent autobiography *Winning*[8] he cites many examples that contributed to England being crowned world champions.

An interesting thing happened four years later when France staged the 2007 Rugby World Cup. When the French realised at the outset of the tournament that they could meet the legendary All-Blacks in the final they changed their bright royal blue jersey to a very dark blue. Why? The television companies around the world would insist on one team changing their jerseys to avoid a clash of colours and as the home nation France would be allowed to wear their jersey in the final while the New Zealanders would have to change their famous black jersey. How less powerful would an All-Blacks team playing in their second strip of all white be in a World Cup final? All very psychological, but a great example of the lengths sporting teams will go just to find that one little thing that could make the difference between winning and losing. Ironically, it didn't come to pass as neither France nor the All-Blacks reached the final.

The way you do the little things will say a lot about the way you will do the big things.

Focus on the little things. Winners always do.

Because it is the little things that often make the difference between winning and losing.

The way you do the little things says a lot about the way you will do the big things

I found out that there weren't too many limitations if I did it my way.

Johnny Cash

FAN YOUR FLAME

Winners display passion. Why do so many people lose their passion in life? Maybe it is greed, dwelling on things you don't have so that you don't enjoy the things you do have. Or perhaps it's fear — running from things that are not chasing you and so robbing yourself of inner peace and stability and tormenting yourself with the "what ifs". Or could it be seeking fulfilment in the wrong places?

It is those with the greatest passion who succeed. Passionate people with limited ability will outperform passive people with ability because they act with boundless enthusiasm. Passionate people take risks, go that extra mile, do what it takes to achieve their goals (no matter how often they fail) and don't stop until they succeed. Passionate people will persevere until they find what they are looking for and won't be deterred by those who pour scorn on their efforts.

Think of a flame. Are you a person with a low flame? It's difficult to achieve anything when you don't have much desire to do so. So find something you like to do so much that you'll gladly do it for nothing, and if you learn to do it well, some day people will gladly pay you for it. Or are you a person with no flame? Do you say you are burned out when if you are totally honest you never really were ever on fire? Or are you a person with a flame? You refuse to allow anyone, or anything, to stand in your way. Your passion is matched with your priorities and you do not waste your time doing things that demand neither passion nor talent.

Align your passion with your priorities. Fan your flame, regularly; otherwise it will tend to go out. Feed it. Protect it. And remember — not everyone will help you do that. So you need to distinguish between two sorts of people. Seek out the firelighters — people who inspire you, encourage you, and will go out of their way to help you. They see you not just as you are, but also as you could be, and in doing so fuel your faith and ignite your passion. Beware of fire extinguishers — people who throw cold water on what you are trying to achieve. They focus on what's wrong rather than what's right, will find the cloud that comes with every silver lining, and will try to put out the fire of your passion.

So, look out for firelighters and spend time with them and you will find that as you fan the flames, the flames will energise you and carry you to your destination.

Passionate people with limited ability will outperform passive people with ability because they act with boundless enthusiasm.

Man doesn't know what he is capable of until he is asked.

Kofi Annan

BIG – BIGGER – BEST

At eight minutes past eight on the eighth day of the eighth month of the year 2008, the Beijing Olympics were declared open. When China was awarded the Olympic Games seven years earlier they said they would stage a spectacle never seen before. They didn't disappoint.

With a potential television audience of billions it was the biggest and the most costly opening ceremony in the history of the games and is unlikely to be ever matched again. Fourteen thousand performers, 2008 drummers playing the fou – a Chinese percussion instrument – in perfect unison, 29 giant firework "footprints" – representing the number of modern Olympic Games – which were set off in locations from the centre of Beijing to the stadium and a three minute display involving 30,000 fireworks that almost defied imagination. The climax, the lighting of the Olympic flame, was the piece de resistance, the torchbearer whisked on wires around the very eaves of the gigantic Bird's Nest stadium. The three-hour ceremony was so stunningly choreographed, so meticulously planned (full dress rehearsals began more than a year previous) it was one of the greatest shows the world has seen.

China is the new emerging power on the world stage. Their staging of the Olympic Games, at a cost of $43 billion, was their opportunity to show what having a winning mindset looks like. They truly lived up to the mark.

It was one of the greatest shows the world has seen.

Successful people are simply those with successful habits.

Brian Tracy

THE 7 HABITS THAT CAN STOP YOU WINNING

What's stopping you being a winner? Sometimes it is our habits that hold us back. Our thinking guides our beliefs and our beliefs sow the seeds of our habits. Our habits can quickly become routine that is repeated regularly and tends to occur unconsciously.

Are you guilty of any of these?

1. **Passing judgement**: Remember, your judgements don't define others; they define you.

2. **Making excuses**: It is said that 99% of failures come from people who have the habit of making excuses.

3. **Refusing to express regret**: The most powerful phrase in the English language is "I'm sorry". Use it when you have to.

4. **Failure to express gratitude**: Research shows that the number one reason why people become disillusioned and underperform in the workplace is because of a lack of recognition and appreciation.

5. **Passing the buck**: When you pass the buck you fail to take responsibility.

6. **Using "but"**: "But" is a horrible word. Remember, any sentence with "but" in the middle of it – all the words before it are a waste of space.

7. **Clinging to the past**: The only time you should look back is to look forward.

There is no secret formula for changing habits. To change our habits we need to change our thinking. When we change our thinking we can change our beliefs.

Your judgements don't define others; they define you.

There are many tomorrows, my love, my love. There is only one today.

Joaquin Miller

APPRECIATE THE MOMENT

We live in a culture of wanting everything now. To wait is to be left behind. Modern lifestyle dictates that time is precious and yet happiness is defined, in part at least, as having the desire and ability to sacrifice what we want now for what we want eventually. Today's world is one where people have more of everything, except time. Having more doesn't make us happier. If it did there would be less unhappy millionaires in the world.

Moments are special. They are to be enjoyed. Do you remember your first kiss? Or buying your first record? Life, itself, is all about key moments. Older generations know exactly where they were and what they were doing when Kennedy was shot or when Neil Armstrong stepped on to the moon. Many of us can remember where we were when hearing of the death of Princess Diana or when the planes struck the Twin Towers.

Many of us get caught up in the busyness of life. We get "hurry sickness".

Here are some of the symptoms:

- If you are microwaving something for 30 seconds, you have to do something else while waiting for the timer to ping.
- You eat at your desk while checking your email and are often on the phone at the same time.
- You hate the time it takes to boot up your computer so much that you never turn it off.
- You turn on your smartphone as soon as your plane lands – before you are meant to – and get stressed out by how long it takes to get a signal.
- You repeatedly press the "door close" as soon as you get into the lift.

Enjoy now. It will never come again.

Today's world is one where people have more of everything, except time.

Recognition is the greatest motivator.

Gerard C. Eakedale

MAKE OTHERS FEEL IMPORTANT

The real reason why people are interested in winners is because winners are interested in people.

If you really want to get to know someone, ask him or her this one thing - describe your perfect day.

It is believed Winston Churchill once said, "I don't like that man; I must get to know him." Think of someone you don't like. How well do you know them? Maybe when you get to know them you will like them.

John Dewey, one of America's most profound philosophers, said that the deepest urge in human nature is "the desire to be important." In recent years we have had numerous examples of wealthy individuals from Russia, Asia and the Middle East buying up English Premiership football clubs. For many of these individuals their purchase was not based on a love of football but rather the need to feel important.

NASA spent millions back in the 1960s in their attempt to be the first to put a man on the moon. Hours of preparation went into making sure everything would go smoothly in order to achieve one of man's greatest feats. But the biggest dilemma facing NASA was deciding which astronaut would be the first to walk on the moon. It is believed both Neil Armstrong and Buzz Aldrin wanted to be the one that made that "one small step for man, one giant leap for mankind" because everyone would remember who it was that made that first step on to another world.

Make others feel important.

Winners always do.

The real reason why people are interested in winners is because winners are interested in people.

Gratitude is a sometime thing in this world.

Just because you've been feeding them all winter, don't expect the birds to take it easy on your grass seed.

Bill Vaughan.

THE PRICE OF APPRECIATION

There was a blind girl who hated herself because she was blind. She hated
everyone, except her loving boyfriend. He was always there for her.

She told her boyfriend, "If I could only see the world, I would marry you."

One day, someone donated eyes to her.

Weeks later when the bandages came off, she was able to see everything,
including her boyfriend.

He asked her, "Now that you can see the world, will you marry me?"

The girl looked at her boyfriend and saw that he was blind. The sight of his closed
eyelids shocked her. She hadn't expected that and the thought of looking at them
for the rest of her life led her to refuse his marriage proposal.

Her boyfriend left with a broken heart.

A few days later she received a note from him saying:

"Take good care of your eyes my dear, for before they were yours, they were
mine."

*"Take good care of your eyes my dear, for before they were yours, they were
mine."*

PRINCIPLE 7

ALWAYS WANT TO IMPROVE

What you do today can improve all your tomorrows.

Ralph Marston

KAIZEN – CONTINUOUS IMPROVEMENT

The personal mantra for millions of winners is *kaizen*, a Japanese word for constant and never-ending improvement. This is also the philosophy that underpins modern Japanese businesses. Winners always want to be better. When you aspire to win you always aim to improve on what went before.

We live in a world of rapid change so improving is necessary just to survive. But winning is about more than surviving. It is about wanting to thrive.

Long-term improvement begins with small, manageable steps. There is no quick fix on the path to winning. Persistence is often the single most common quality of a winning mindset. Winners just don't give up. No matter how hard it seems, the longer you persist the more likely your success. Remember, it's always too soon to quit!

Always want to improve because in the real world the prizes go to those who win. Two days after their Champions League Final defeat on penalties in May 2008 Chelsea manager Avram Grant was sacked. His predecessor, Jose Mourinho, in referring to Grant's sacking said, "In football *almost* means defeat and Chelsea almost won the Carling Cup, almost won the Champions League and almost won the Premiership. Almost is nothing."

This thinking is brilliantly summed up in a quotation from Professor John West-Burnham:

"A quality organisation is restless, constantly questioning, never satisfied, challenging norms believing that things can always be better."

Winners always want to be better.

Everything you want is just outside your comfort zone.

Robert Allen

(co-author: The One Minute Millionaire)

GET OUT OF YOUR COMFORT ZONE

Reflect for a moment on the word "zone" in the phrase "comfort zone". Zone defines a marked space or area. It is the space that contains all your don'ts and cant's and nevers. Are you stuck in your comfort zone of "I can't" or "I couldn't"? An important concept that winners understand is that you are never stuck. To be a winner demands thinking differently, feeling differently and acting differently. It is about thinking outside the box when the box is your comfort zone. Albert Einstein said the significant problems we face cannot be solved by the same level of thinking that created them.

We all have similar comfort zones for the foods we buy in supermarkets, the restaurants we eat in, the kind of car we drive. Our comfort zones change when we are prepared to try something different. Call it risk taking, being creative or pushy but that's why winners are never stuck. Winners only ever move forward and upwards - to where the magic happens.

Where does your magic happen?

Winners only ever move forward and upwards - to where the magic happens.

Always do what you are afraid to do.

Ralph Waldo Emerson

CONFRONT YOUR FEARS

In striving to win you have to confront your fears. Whenever you take on something new there is usually fear. You are outside your comfort zone. Winners feel the fear like everyone else, but with a difference. They don't let fear keep them from doing anything they want to do, or have to do. They understand that fear is something to be acknowledged and experienced.

Almost all our fears are self-created. Mark Twain said, "I have lived a long life and had many troubles, most of which never happened." New experiences will always feel a little scary. They're supposed to. But once you face a fear and do it anyway, you build up so much more confidence in your abilities.

A number of years ago I enrolled for swimming lessons. On the very first night the instructor took the group to the deep end of the pool and said "You are each going to jump in and you will catch the end of the pole I am holding when you re-surface at the top of the water. I want to get rid of your fear of water." Guess what? It worked.

Crocodile Dundee was a hugely successful movie for actor Paul Hogan. Hogan says "The secret to my success is that I bit off more than I could chew and chewed as fast as I could." In 1998 the then Secretary of State for Northern Ireland, Mo Mowlam, went into the Maze Prison to talk to the prisoners in an effort to move the Northern Ireland peace process forward. Many believed Mowlam was biting off more than she could chew. In her autobiography, *Momentum*, she talks about how she needed to be courageous to overcome others' fears. It is generally accepted that Mo Mowlam's prison visit was a seminal moment in bringing peace to Northern Ireland.

Things happen when you confront your fears.

Fear is something to be acknowledged and experienced.

The man who views the world at 50 the same as he did at 20 has wasted 30 years of his life.

Muhammad Ali

DON'T TAKE "NO" FOR AN ANSWER

To be a winner entails being able to deal with rejection. Rejection is a natural part of life. You experience rejection when you aren't picked for the team, don't get the promotion at work, or your offer of a date is turned down. Don't let rejection stop you.

The secret to winning is to learn to accept rejection. Too many people throw in the towel too early. When someone says no just move on and try again. Life is a numbers game. To win in life, business, and everything else means to keep asking and looking until you get the yes you are looking for.

Sometimes things just don't work out. If you've tried everything possible and it just hasn't worked out as planned, stop trying so hard. Relax. Maybe nothing's wrong. Maybe the timing's not right. Maybe what you wanted wasn't in your best interests.

Life teaches us that not all poems are meant to rhyme. A lot of life is about making the most of now because we don't know what's going to happen tomorrow, or next week.

Clients often ask me, "How do you know when to quit?" Sometimes you get to a point where you just know it's time to change tack. You just *know*. I often say that when that time comes, you will know. You feel it in your bones like a sixth sense.

Do your best and let life do the rest.

Life teaches us that not all poems are meant to rhyme.

Paralyse resistance with your persistence.

Woody Hughes

BE PERSISTENT

To be a winner means having high expectations – of yourself, and of others. In turn, you will have high standards. High expectations are easy: their realisation is not. This demands time, commitment and patience. Winners never compromise on their expectations or their standards – never.

Being consistent about your expectations also means being persistent. People can often do more than you think they can. When you insist on the very best in people's work, you often encounter resistance because doing the very best requires hard work. If you let people be less than their best, they generally do not actively resist. So it sometimes seems that they would rather do less than their best. Insist on the best and you'll get the best. Reminds me of the lovely story in Ken Blanchard's book *The One Minute Manager Meets The Monkey*[3] about the farmer who, when asked by his neighbour why he was working his sons so hard just to grow corn, replied "I'm not just growing corn. I'm growing sons."

Insist on the best and you'll get the best.

Feedback is the breakfast of champions.

Ken Blanchard

EMBRACE FEEDBACK

There are two kinds of feedback – negative and positive. Interestingly research shows us that we tend to gravitate towards negative feedback. I have found this to be my experience. When I collect and collate the evaluation forms from my training workshops I tend to scan for those evaluations that contain negative feedback even though the ratio might be 1:25. We prefer positive feedback. It makes us feel better. It tells us that we are doing the right thing. We tend not to like negative feedback but our natural instinct is to search it out first. However, there is often more useful data in negative feedback than in positive feedback. Negative feedback tells me how I can improve what I am doing. To have a winning mindset you need to welcome, receive and embrace all the feedback that comes your way.

Feedback is simply information. Be open to feedback. It is a gift that helps you to be more effective. Sometimes not all feedback is useful or accurate. You must consider the source. Some feedback is distorted by the mood, mindset or general attitude of the giver of the feedback at any given time. More importantly, look for patterns in the feedback you get. If several people are telling you the same thing, there is probably some truth in it.

When you are the giver of feedback always start with a positive. If you can't see a positive, find one. Always make people feel good about themselves. When we suggest a better way or a different way to do things always highlight what the benefit will be when the receiver embraces your suggestion. People act when they have a motive or a compelling reason to act – so be compelling. Winners always are.

We tend to gravitate towards negative feedback.

To ask is to always seek knowledge.

(advice from my Maths O-Level teacher)

ASK AND YOU WILL RECEIVE

It never hurts to ask. Asking for help is a true sign of maturity. Asking for help should not be seen as a weakness. It is a source of strength. Yet why are so many people afraid to ask? They are afraid of being made look foolish or stupid. But mostly they are afraid of rejection, of hearing the word *no*. In reality, they are actually rejecting themselves in advance. They're saying no to themselves before anyone else even has a chance to.

Someone else has already done almost everything you want to do. There are loads of people who are available as mentors, advisors, coaches and consultants. Talk to them – write, phone or visit. Most people love to talk about how they accomplished their goals or got to the top. They can only talk if you ask.

In order to be a winner you need to take advantage of all the resources available to you. There are always reasons why we don't – it's too inconvenient, I might get rejected, or it's too much hard work. Find out what made others successful. Find someone who has already done what you want to do and meet them for a chat. And make sure to ask them all the right questions and the "right" questions are always open questions – what, when, where, who, why, and how?

Winners ask, all the time. And the more you do it, the easier it gets.

Nothing happens until you ask.

Asking for help is a true sign of maturity.

Believe in better.

(BSkyB strapline)

WAS LIFE BETTER?

Today is the past that somebody in the future will be longing to go back to. Do you agree?

Remember the time when you could go out to play at 9 in the morning until 6 in the evening and not ever get a text message to ask where you are.

Was life better? Would you like to go back? I once heard a wise old man say that it would be wonderful to go back to yesterday - with today's knowledge.

Reflect on this question - if you didn't know what age you are, what age would you like to be? And why?

Life in the past may or may not have been better but it was simpler. Life today is complicated, fast, and uncertain. We have more choice, and with more choice we have more responsibility. We now live in a world where the pace of change outstrips our capacity to digest and comprehend it fully. Such is the pace of change that most of the jobs our children will do have not even been created yet.

The winners in life, business, and everything else embrace change and always see change as an opportunity. For those who fear change the difficulty is more often about letting go of the past rather than embracing the future.

In 2012 the British Olympic Association coined the phrase *better never stops* as their strapline for the 2012 London Olympics.

Better never stops – the mindset of a winner.

Better never stops.

Let's go invent tomorrow instead of worrying what happened yesterday.

Steve Jobs

A DIGITAL DINOSAUR OR A FUTURE OPPORTUNIST?

In the past two months did you do any of these?

Read Yellow Pages

Use public phone

Put an ad in the shop window

Record things using VHS

Dial directory enquiries

Ring the cinema to find out times

Ring the speaking clock

Write a letter by hand

Own an encyclopaedia

Fax something

Pay by cheque

Send a postcard

Carry portable CD players

Ring 1471

Go to the travel agents to research a holiday

Are you someone who finds it difficult to let go of the past?

Or are you a future opportunist who is excited by the many opportunities that the future holds?

Remember an opportunity is never lost. It is just found by someone else.

An opportunity is never lost. It is just found by someone else.

Always turn a negative situation into a positive situation.

Michael Jordan

DON'T FEED THE HORSES

There is a man who lives beside me and he owns some horses. It so happens that the school bus stops right at the gate to his horses' field and, while he is at work, the school children feed the horses their scraps.

The horses love it. Mars Bars, crisps and stuff the kids had made in cookery class. The horses even developed a taste for pepperoni pizza. Over time, the horses got fat. So the man put up a sign that said:

Do not feed the horses.

Did it work? Most definitely not! The feeding continued, so the owner changed the sign. It now read:

Please do not feed the horses!

But his problem continued. He didn't know what to do.

One day he approached me and said:

"JJ, I know you do a lot of work around positive psychology and I have a problem." He explained the problem in the hope of getting a simple solution. *"How on earth can I stop the kids feeding my horses?"*

"Very simple" I replied and I wrote him a few words on a scrap of paper. My neighbour looked at the piece of paper and laughed.

"No way!" he said, and as he walked away shaking his head I smiled a knowing smile because I knew the problem was cured.

The horses are now back to their normal weight, their coats shining and energy restored. If you saunter past their field there is now a sign that says:

We only eat apples and carrots.

The message is simple and positive. It focuses on what we want to happen rather than what we don't want.

And best of all, it works.

It focuses on what we want to happen rather than what we don't want.

We were born to make manifest the glory of God that is within us.

It's not just in some of us; it's in everyone.

And as we let our own light shine, we unconsciously give other people permission to do the same.

Marianne Williamson

THE 4 QUESTIONS EVERY WINNER ASKS

As a winner you won't have all the answers but you must ask all the right questions – and there are four questions every winner asks:

Q1. What are **the good things** I do I must continue doing?

Q2. What are **the bad things** I do I must stop doing?

Q3. What are **the occasional things** I do I must do more often?

Q4. What are **the things I don't do** I must start doing?

When we know our "what", we can plan our "how", and understand our "why".

Remember, there are two great days in a person's life – the day they are born and the day they discover why.

Winners, they've discovered why.

There are two great days in a person's life – the day they are born and the day they discover why.

THE 15 REASONS WHY WINNERS WIN

THE 15 REASONS WHY WINNERS WIN

1. Winners have a winning mindset – that becomes a winning habit.
2. Winners are 6F thinkers – they see the bigger picture.
3. Winners do the little things that others don't value as much – and do them well.
4. Winners believe in themselves when no one else does.
5. Winners do what losers don't do – they set goals.
6. Winners know that setting goals is a statement that you refuse to be ordinary.
7. Winners recognise that the biggest impediment to winning is inherited thinking.
8. Winners champion their potential and aim to go where others don't dare.
9. Winners see mistakes as opportunities for learning.
10. Winners understand that practice is the price a winner pays to be called a winner.
11. Winners know that winning is about getting good at being uncomfortable.
12. Winners understand that winning is about rising above social approval to self-approval.
13. Winners realise that when you give people what they want but in a way they least expect then you are on to a winner.
14. Winners recognise that better never stops.
15. Winners have discovered WHY.

Download Your FREE Bonus Chapter NOW!

Barack Obama's

3 Winning Secrets

Simply put the word **BARACK** in your subject title and send your email to:

info@leadingedgeleadership.com

Endnotes

1. Bodenhamer, Bob, and Hall, Michael, *The User Manual for the Brain*, Crown House Publishing, Carmarthen, 1999

2. Covey, Stephen R, *The 7 Habits of Highly Effective People*, Simon and Schuster, 1989

3. Frankl, Viktor E, *Man's Search For Meaning*, Simon and Schuster, 1959

4. Carroll, Lewis, *Alice in Wonderland*, Wordsworth Editions Ltd, 1992

5. Sinek, Simon, *Start With Why*, Penguin, 2011

6. Dale Carnegie, *How to Win Friends and Influence People*, Simon and Schuster, 1936

7. Hall, Richard, *The Secrets of Success at Work*, Prentice Hall Business, 2008

8. Woodward, Clive, *Winning!* Hodder Paperbacks, 2004

9. Blanchard, Ken, *The One Minute Manager Meets The Monkey*, Harper, 1990

ABOUT THE AUTHOR

JJ Lynch is an international leadership trainer, facilitator, coach, author and motivational speaker.

He is Managing Director of Leading Edge Leadership (www.leadingedgeleadership.com), a leadership training company specialising in motivational leadership, people development and organisational change.

JJ is always in big demand across the world as a trainer and as a motivational speaker. He regularly facilitates workshops and team away days and frequently acts as Master of Ceremonies (MC) at large-scale events.

JJ's anecdotal style, his use of multimedia, and his ability to relate the content of his work to real life insights and practical everyday examples make for a truly engaging learning experience.

Leading Edge LEADERSHIP

making leadership easy

for all your leadership training needs

leadership training programmes

bite-sized leadership workshops

leadership coaching

motivational leadership talks

facilitation of away days, events and meetings

EMAIL: info@leadingedgeleadership.com

Leading Edge LEADERSHIP
making leadership easy

Our Complete Range of
Leadership and Management Programmes

CORE LEADERSHIP AND MANAGEMENT PROGRAMMES (2 DAYS)

Managers The Highly Effective Manager	Leaders The Highly Effective Leader	Senior Leaders The Executive Leadership Programme	All Leaders/Managers The Complete Leadership and Management Programme (5 Days)

CORE SKILLS PROGRAMMES (2 DAYS)

Advanced Communication and Presentation Skills for Leaders	The Highly Effective Presenter	The Highly Effective Trainer

FINE TUNING YOUR SKILLS (2 DAYS)

Developing Your People Management Skills	Developing Your Personal Brand	Influencing and Persuading Skills	Developing Team Performance	Writing Effective Reports

FINE TUNING YOUR SKILLS (1 DAY)

Appraisal Skills – Managing Performance	Assertiveness Skills	Coaching Skills for Better Performance
Communicating Effectively in The Workplace	Conflict Resolution	Creativity and Innovation
Creative Problem Solving	Dealing with Difficult People	Delegation Skills
Effective Meeting Skills	Emotional Intelligence	Event Management
Managing Pressure and Competing Demands	Strategy – The Key to Successful Leadership	Presenting with Confidence
Project Management – An Introduction	Introduction to Customer Care and Handling Customer Complaints	Managing Challenging Situations for Managers
Managing Change	Excelling in Leadership	Negotiation Skills
NLP – An Introduction	Facilitation Skills	Interviewing Skills
Selling Skills	Excelling in Management	Stress Management
Supervision Skills	Talent Management	Team Leader Skills
Time Management Skills	Train the Trainer (for new trainers)	Women in Management and Leadership

FINE TUNING YOUR SKILLS FURTHER

40 Bite–Sized Leadership Workshops (90 minutes each)	Motivational Leadership Talks (10 Great New Talks)	Leadership Coaching (1/2/3 hours sessions)	Facilitation of Away Days, Events and Meetings

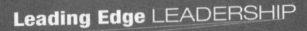

Leading Edge LEADERSHIP

making leadership easy

The **"Making Leadership Easy"** Series
of

40
"HOW TO"
BITE-SIZED
Leadership Workshops

90 MINUTES EACH
HIGHLY FOCUSED
COVERS THE ESSENTIALS

GREATER
CHOICE

GREATER
FLEXIBILITY

UP TO
25 DELEGATES
CAN ATTEND EACH
WORKSHOP

UP TO 4 WORKSHOPS
IN A DAY

... for all your leadership training needs

"How To" Bite-Sized Leadership Workshop Titles

How to Be Assertive

How to Negotiate

How to Delegate

How to Motivate

How to Manage Conflict

How to Facilitate

How to Market Yourself

How to Influence and Persuade

How to Lead Teams

How to Communicate Better

How to Manage Performance

How to Manage Change

How to Think Strategically

How to Be Interesting

How to Coach One-to-One

How to Run Effective Meetings

How to Lead Difficult People

How to Manage Talent

How to Manage Stress

How to Manage A Project

How to Start Up and Lead A Successful Business

How to Create A Happy Productive Workplace

How to Improve Your Selling Skills

How to Write An Effective Report

How to Run Effective Events

How to Interview Successfully

How to Succeed At An Assessment Centre

How to Excel As A Leader

How to Excel As A Manager

How to Run An Effective Appraisal Meeting

How to Manage Your Manager

How to Find Creative Solutions to Problems

How to Be The Best You Can Be

How to Make The Perfect Presentation

How to Develop Your Emotional Intelligence

How to Develop Excellent Customer Care

How to Improve Your Memory Skills

How to Manage Your Time Better

How to Improve Your Listening Skills

How to Tell Stories to Inspire and Motivate

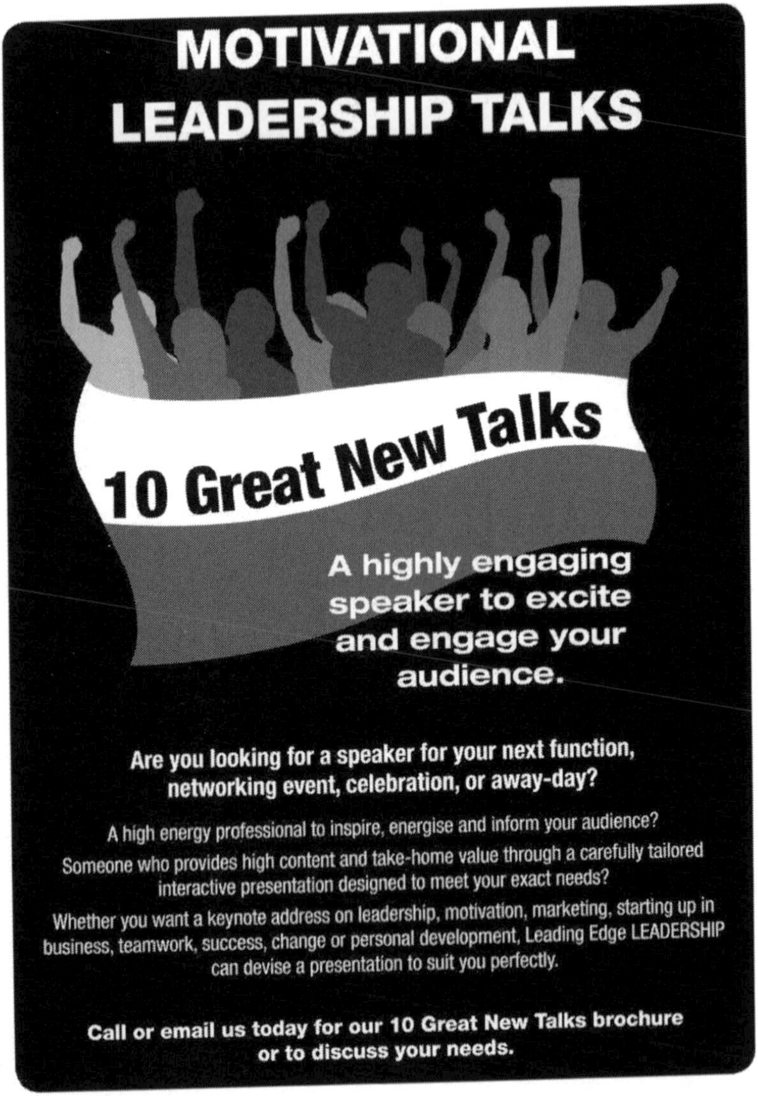
MOTIVATIONAL
LEADERSHIP TALKS
10 Great New Talks
A highly engaging speaker to excite and engage your audience.
Are you looking for a speaker for your next function, networking event, celebration, or away-day?
A high energy professional to inspire, energise and inform your audience?
Someone who provides high content and take-home value through a carefully tailored interactive presentation designed to meet your exact needs?
Whether you want a keynote address on leadership, motivation, marketing, starting up in business, teamwork, success, change or personal development, Leading Edge LEADERSHIP can devise a presentation to suit you perfectly.
Call or email us today for our 10 Great New Talks brochure or to discuss your needs.

MOTIVATIONAL TALK SUMMARIES

Talk 1

The Privilege of Leadership

*The unusual combination of
attributes for effective leadership*

Talk 2

How To Make Your Business Stand Out From The Crowd

The search for difference

Talk 3

How to Win

in life, business, and everything else

Talk 4

What Makes Successful People Successful

*How the most successful business
leaders think, act, and achieve*

Talk 5

Unleashing The Leadership Potential Of Your People

*How to get the very best from your
people all day, every day*

Talk 6

How To Lead Your Business To Success

*What the most successful business leaders
know, do, say, see, hear, and look like*

Talk 7

The Making Of Champions

*The 3 key leadership lessons from
the world of sport to get your
business to No.1*

Talk 8

Transformational Leadership the Obama Way

*The 3 key messages for all successful
business leaders*

Talk 9

Leadership For Growth

*Grow leaders –
grow your results*

Talk 10

Brilliant You

*7 principles for self-leadership
and achievement*

Made in the USA
Charleston, SC
19 July 2016